SOMETHING OF A SAINT

David Maldwyn Owen was brought up in Haverfordwest, Dyfed. He is now a Minister in the United Reformed Church in Reigate, Surrey and also works part-time as a hospital chaplain. From 1981 to 1990 he wrote a religious column in *Woman's Weekly* magazine which reached a readership of several million. He writes regularly for the International Bible Reading Association and his previous books have included poetry, hymns and church liturgy.

Almighty God,
You call your witnesses from every nation
and reveal your glory in their lives.
Make us thankful for their example
and strengthen us by their fellowship
that we, like them, may be faithful
   in the service of your kingdom;
through Jesus Christ our Lord.

Collect for Group Commemorations, ASB 1980

DAVID M OWEN

Something of a Saint

The Lives and Prayers of Fifty-two Famous Christians

'I was seated next to a Calcutta socialite who was discussing her latest charity. I asked her if she had heard of Mother Teresa. She paused, looked quizzically surprised, and said, "Yes, I have, actually. She's something of a saint, isn't she?" '

DESMOND DOIG

Mother Teresa: Her People and Her Work

First published 1990
Triangle
SPCK
Holy Trinity Church
Marylebone Road
London NW1 4DU

British Library Cataloguing in Publication Data

Owen, David M. (David Maldwyn) 1934–
Something of a saint.
1. Saints. Biographies. Collections
I. Title
270

ISBN 0-281-04481-3

Typeset by Inforum Typesetting, Portsmouth
Printed in Great Britain by
BPCC Hazell Books
Aylesbury, Bucks

Contents

Dedicated to
The memory of my grandfather
ABEL HUGHES
a 'saint' in his day who nurtured
me in Christ when I was
a child

Introduction

When John Buchan came to write a tribute to the memory of one of his close friends he realized how hard it would be to summarize the larger-than-life personality in a short biographical sketch:

> It is not easy to draw on a little canvas the man whose nature is large and central and human, without cranks or oddities. The very simplicity and wholesomeness of such souls defy an easy summary, for they are as spacious in their effect as daylight or summer.

I have had the same experience in writing this book. All fifty-two characters that make up its contents lived spacious lives, and need more biographical space than can be allowed them here, and, in one sense, they do not fit into any book, however large, for their personalities and accomplishments, to say nothing of their faith and their God, are far greater than we can imagine. They belong to life's immeasurables; they fit no neat statistics; their influence on the Church and the world defies calculation; they are immortal, and belong to all of us of every age who belong to Christ.

They would doubtless dispute any glowing evaluation of themselves. Indeed, a feature common to them all is their deep sense of unworthiness before God, as several of their confessional prayers show. They were men and women of their day, subject to temptations and pressures to which they sometimes yielded; but they were acutely aware of the grace of God by which they were called and equipped, and they depended on prayer to sustain them. They were human enough to suffer periods of spiritual drought and a lessening of faith, and that brings them closer to us than if they were superhuman figures, which is a commonly held but naive view of the Christian saints. One schoolgirl described the saints as 'a breed of super-spiritual men who flourished in the Middle-Ages, but which is now extinct. They grew long beards, wore haloes, sprouted wings and spent their time playing harps.' I cannot see that remotely applying to any of the saints in this book!

An explanation at this point regarding 'saints'. Of the fifty-two listed names, twenty-eight are officially called saints, having been canonized by the Church in recognition of their outstanding spirituality and contribution. The other twenty-four received no such accolade (though I like to think Mother Teresa will in time), but they are all 'saints' in the New Testament sense of that word. Where the Authorised Version of the Bible records the apostle Paul writing to 'the saints' at Ephesus and Colossae, the New English Bible calls them simply 'God's people', that is the congregation or membership in each place. I like both descriptions. Most of us have known people in our churches we can quite happily call 'saints' because of their loving and generous ways. Another child wrote more accurately, after seeing a saint portrayed in a stained-glass window, 'a saint is someone the light shines through'. There is a good deal of truth in that.

What characterizes a saint? I suggest that a saint is someone who exhibits Paul's 'fruits of the Spirit' – 'love, joy, peace, patience, kindness, goodness, fidelity, gentleness and self-control' (Galations 5.22 NEB). Add to these features courage, perseverance, cheerfulness and the extra mile, especially under conditions of hardship and persecution, and apply them in general to the characters in this book, and we will see that these people are more than worthy to be called 'saints'. Their hallmark is their likeness to Christ who displayed all these attributes.

Selecting fifty-two famous names across the centuries was no easy task. And you may query the list! Have I omitted your favourite saint? Your most admired Christian? Some are missing that I would otherwise have included – Saint David, for example, so dear to my Celtic heart and homeland – but he like many others never left a personal prayer (at least so far as my research goes), and that, added to an interesting life story, has determined the scope of this book. To a large extent they have chosen themselves by placing their prayers on record, and that absolves me somewhat over the matter of omissions! Also, only ten of the fifty-two are women, but for the same reason.

The choice was made also with a view to variety. The entire list includes archbishops, bishops, martyrs, scholars, writers, monks, nuns, mystics, missionaries, Reformers, Dissenters, preachers, pastors, poets, a cardinal, a king, a nurse and a civil rights leader, thus indicating the boundless diversity of Christian opinion, doctrine, churchmanship and life-style over 2,000 years. Some held viewpoints poles apart, like those of Ignatius Loyola and John Bunyan, but they all served Christ as they felt led, often in the face of bitter opposition. And they all helped to correct trends in the Church which had led it off course in a particular direction. In the light of St Paul's description of the Church as the Body of Christ in which each part functions for the good of the whole (1 Corinthians 12.12–31), we can conclude that neither Catholic nor Protestant, theologian nor activist, bishop nor Dissenter, can say they have no need of each other. They are certainly different, but where it matters they are one – one in the faith of Christ and in their earnest zeal to further his kingdom on earth. Thankfully, no single denomination has a monopoly of saintliness.

If we are open to the leading of the Spirit each 'saint' should challenge us in one way or another toward a deeper commitment to Christ. I find that their devotion, mingled with their humanity, makes the spiritual journey exciting and encouraging, and its end seems more easily attainable. They are a spur to us who are today's 'saints in Caesar's household', ever struggling and learning. The devout Mother Julian of Norwich dispels the notion that the spiritual journey was the specialized activity of a few exceptionally good people: 'There is nothing very special about seeking. It is a thing that every soul can do with God's grace . . . So I saw him and sought him; I had him and wanted him. It seems to me that this is and should be an experience common to us all.' And Ignatius Loyola was greatly encouraged when he read the saints, remarking that since they were as human as he was he knew he could be as saintly as they were.

The 'saints' in this collection would say, I feel sure, that if they achieved anything for God it was through prayer. It was this combination of their life and their prayer that aroused my interest for this book, and I trust it will help strengthen our living and praying.

David Maldwyn Owen
Reigate 1990

ST CLEMENT

Date of birth unknown, but died *c.*100

Bishop of Rome; Martyr

FEAST DAY: 23 *November (West) or 24 November (East)*

The apostle Paul, writing from Rome to the Philippians, mentions a certain Clement (Phil. 4.3), which has led some people to believe he was the Bishop of Rome by that name. We cannot say for certain, but in one of Clement's own writings he refers to Paul as though he knew him, telling of the apostle's great courage under persecution.

Clement would have remained obscure but for his *Epistles to the Corinthians* which were highly regarded by the early Christians. In the first epistle, written in AD 96, he deals firmly with the strife in the Church caused by jealousy among its leaders. Calling for repentance and reconciliation, he reminds his readers that God has appointed bishops and deacons in each place, and it is they who lay down the pattern of ministry in the Church. This early insight into church life and ministry is of considerable value to us.

He wrote movingly:

The strong must make sure that they care for the weak. The rich must be certain to give enough to supply all the needs of the poor. The poor must thank God for supplying their needs. . . . We all need each other: the great need the small, the small need the great. In our body the head is useless without the feet and the feet without the head. The tiniest limbs of our body are useful and necessary to the whole.

1

It is believed Clement was exiled to the Crimea by the Emperor Trajan as punishment for the powerful influence of his work in Rome. He was imprisoned and made to do manual labour in the mines, but nothing diminished his witness for Christ, and he converted many to Christianity.

Tradition says Clement met his death by being thrown into the sea with an anchor tied around his neck, which explains why he is represented by the emblem of the anchor in Christian art, and also why he is patron of Trinity House, the authority responsible for lighthouses and lightships.

The church of St Clement Danes in London is the most famous of the forty or so churches dedicated to him in Britain, having been originally named so by the Danes.

Clement gave us a short and lovely prayer, which was no doubt in keeping with his outlook and way of life:

O God, make us children of
quietness, and heirs of peace.

Almighty God, Father of Jesus Christ our Lord, establish and confirm us in your truth by your Holy Spirit in our hearts. Reveal to us what we do not know, replenish in us what we lack, enrich in us the knowledge we have, and keep us faultless in your service, through the same Jesus Christ our Lord.

We ask you, Lord and Master, to be our help and defence. Relieve the oppressed, raise the fallen, comfort the lonely, heal the sick, feed the hungry, be merciful to the ungodly, and convert your wandering people. Make us pure with your cleansing truth, and lead us in the ways of holiness and singleness of heart. Make your face to shine upon us in peace, and save us from all our sins.

ST POLYCARP

c.69–c.155

Bishop of Smyrna; Martyr

FEAST DAY: *23 February (formerly 26 January)*

As a disciple of John the Evangelist and Bishop of Smyrna for many years, Polycarp was an important Christian leader in the mid-second-century Church in Asia Minor. He was a defender of the faith against Gnostic heresies, and had as his pupils the notable Church Fathers Irenaeus and Papias.

Returning from Smyrna to Rome, where he had conferred with Bishop Anicetus over such matters as the date for celebrating Easter, Polycarp was arrested during an outburst of persecution against the Christians under Marcus Aurelius. Facing his captors with calmness and courage, he invited them to eat at his table while he withdrew for an hour to pray.

At his interrogation before the proconsul Quadratus, Polycarp was advised to consider his age (he was in his eighties), to swear an oath of allegiance to Caesar and to revile Christ. He replied

> For eighty-six years I have served him and he has done me no wrong; how can I blaspheme my King and Saviour? If you require me to swear by the genius of Caesar, as you call it, hear my confession. I am a Christian, and if you desire to learn the Christian doctrines, choose a time and hear me.

He spoke with such conviction and grace that his appearance seemed to shine, impressing everyone around, including the proconsul. Polycarp was sentenced to death. The crowd at the games in the amphitheatre called for him to be thrown to the lions, but instead he was burned alive over a pile of wood. He refused to be nailed to the stake: 'It is unnecessary,' he said, 'for he who gives me strength to endure in the flame will enable me to stand firm.'

He died praising and praying to God. The flames, it is said, formed themselves like the sails of a ship billowing in the wind, and gently encircled the body of the martyr.

The account of Polycarp's death is of particular interest since it is among the earliest records we have of Christian martyrdom outside the New Testament. Countless similar atrocities followed under the Roman Caesars until the Emperor Constantine gave Christianity official recognition.

Prayers before his death

Lord God, Father of Jesus Christ, I praise you for counting me worthy of this day and hour, for numbering me among the martyrs and allowing me to drink the chalice of your Son that I might rise and live eternally in the Holy Spirit. Let me be counted among the martyrs in your presence, a pleasing and acceptable sacrifice. You have faithfully prepared my life for this, and now it is upon me. I praise and glorify you through the eternal High Priest, Jesus Christ, your beloved Son. Through him, with him and the Holy Spirit may glory be yours for ever.

We pray that God the Father, and the eternal High Priest Jesus Christ, may nurture us in faith, truth and love, and grant us our portion among the saints and all who believe in our Lord Jesus Christ. We pray for all the people of Christ, for rulers and leaders, for all the enemies of his cross, and for ourselves that our fruit may increase, and we be made perfect in Christ Jesus our Lord.

ST IRENAEUS

c.130–c.200

Bishop of Lyons; Theologian

FEAST DAY: *28 June (West) or 23 August (East)*

As a boy in the Asia Minor city of Smyrna, Irenaeus was greatly influenced by the life and teaching of the saintly Bishop Polycarp. After studying in Rome he became a priest at Lyons, which was then a flourishing trade centre and the most important bishopric in Gaul (France).

Irenaeus was on a visit to the Pope in Rome when a persecution of Christians broke out at Lyons. Pothinus, Bishop of Lyons, was killed, and on his return to the city Irenaeus was appointed his successor. Irenaeus' achievements as bishop drew the glowing comment of St Gregory of Tours, that his missionary endeavours had within a few years made the whole of Gaul Christian.

Irenaeus was an effective peacemaker. The purpose of his visit to Rome was to ask Pope Eleutherius to deal compassionately with the Montanists, a new and troublesome Pentecostalist-style sect in the Church; not that Irenaeus favoured them, but he made his attempt because he was a mediator at heart. He again acted as peacemaker when the Pope excommunicated those churchmen who celebrated Easter on the same day as the Jewish festival of Passover instead of the Sunday following.

And he was a great Catholic theologian, the first of his kind, who towered over his second-century contemporaries. Although a mediator by nature, he was a clear opponent of the various heresies grouped under the complex religious movement known as Gnosticism, and he spent most of his time refuting them, though always with fairness, courtesy and sound scholarship. His approach was always positive. He emphasized the Church's essential traditions, which were precious to him, as to many today, especially the apostolic episcopate and the importance of the canon of Scripture. He insisted on the authority and trustworthiness of the four Gospels: the Father, Son and Holy Spirit were a unity in the work of revelation and redemption, and the incarnation, he stressed, made Christ fully human.

Irenaeus is believed to have suffered martyrdom, but we cannot be sure. We know he died at Lyons and was buried in the crypt of the church of St John (now Saint Irenée).

We are grateful to him for his writings, which are one of our main sources of information about life and belief in the early Church.

We see in these prayers the strength of Irenaeus' theological thought, his desire that all should come to know the true God, and his loving intercession for all who are striving to live the Christian life.

I pray to you, Lord God of Abraham, Isaac and Jacob, Father of our Lord Jesus Christ. You are infinite in mercy, and it is your will that we should learn to know you. You created heaven and earth, and rule over all. You are the only true God, and there is no other God above you. Grant, through our Lord Jesus Christ, and the working of the Holy Spirit, that all may come to know you, for you alone are God. May all draw strength from you, and all be kept from teaching that is untrue or godless.

O Father, give perfection to beginners,
intelligence to the young ones,
aid to those who are running their course.
Give sorrow to the negligent,
zeal of spirit to the lukewarm,
and to those who have attained, a good ending,
for the sake of Christ Jesus, our Lord.

ST BASIL THE GREAT

c.330–79

Bishop of Caesarea; Theologian

FEAST DAY: 2 *January* (*West*) (*formerly 14 June*)
or 1 January (*East*)

Basil was born at Cappadocia of a deeply Christian family. After a fine education he lived as a hermit in Syria and Egypt and later beside the river Iris in Pontus. But so many people were attracted by his spiritual wisdom that he set up a monastery for them, and thus began his monastic enterprise, following his preference for communal rather than solitary asceticism. 'If you always live alone,' he asked, 'whose feet will you wash?'

Basil drew up strict rules for his monasteries, and was to eastern monasticism what St Benedict was to western. Many of his disciplines are still in force in the East today. It was his trusted friend Gregory of Nazianzum who persuaded Basil to leave the monastery for the outside world where his gifts of preaching and administration were greatly needed. He was already hailed as the champion of orthodox faith against the heresy of Arianism, which denied that Christ was divine, and Basil played a large part in bringing about its later demise.

In the year 370 Basil was made Bishop of Caesarea in Cappadocia, a post he held for the rest of his life. The Arians continued to cause trouble, and he was often in dispute with other parties. But he stood firm in his beliefs and steered the Church through the stormy waters of the time, countering threats of secularism.

By nature Basil was often joyless and despondent,

obsessed with his sinfulness and the woes of the world, though to be fair, constant ill-health was probably a contributing factor. But he was a man of good character and personal holiness and felt a deep concern for the poor and sick. He gave his own money to the needy and organized soup-kitchens for the hungry; alongside churches he built hospitals for the sick and hostels for the homeless, overseeing them personally.

When an angry official once threatened Basil with deprivation, exile and even death, he calmly replied that as he owned but a few rags for clothes, deprivation was no threat; nor was exile since he lived as a stranger in this world, en route for the next; and as for death, that would only result in bringing him closer to God! He was not threatened again.

Thankfully, many of Basil's great thoughts of God have come down to us. Well before the modern space age he believed that God could have made an infinity of worlds and would set no limits to his creative power.

In one of his prayers in which St Basil celebrates Christ's caring attributes, we see a reflection of his own life and work:

O Lord, the help of the helpless,
  the hope of the hopeless,
  the saviour of the storm-tossed,
  the harbour of voyagers,
  the physician of the sick;
We pray to you.
O Lord, you became all things to all men;
  you know each of us and our petitions;
  you know each house and its needs;
Receive us all into your kingdom;
Make us children of light,
And bestow your peace and love upon us.

O Lord my God, teach me to pray for the right blessings. Guide the vessel of my life towards yourself, the tranquil haven for storm-tossed souls. Show me the course I should journey. Renew a willing spirit within me; let your Spirit control my wayward senses; guide me to what is truly good; help me to keep your laws, and in all my works to rejoice in your glory and presence. For yours is the glory and praise of all your saints forever.

ST AMBROSE

*c.*339–97

Bishop of Milan

FEAST DAY: *7 December or 4 April (Book of Common Prayer)*

St Ambrose is called the 'Father of Church Song'. He encouraged hymn-singing by whole congregations and not just by choirs and priests, and his Latin hymns were sung up to the time of the Reformation. Some of them are still in use today in English translations, including 'O Jesus, Lord of heavenly grace'.

Ambrose was born of Christian parents in Gaul, where his father was Praetorian Prefect. After practising law in Rome he became governor of a district which had its seat at Milan, and here he spent the rest of his life, dedicated to the city's spiritual and social welfare.

Trouble followed the death of Milan's Arian bishop, Auxentius, as factions argued about the theological position of his successor, some calling for an Arian, others a Catholic. As Governor Ambrose addressed a gathering on the matter and called for peace, a voice (said to be that of a child) cried out, 'Ambrose for Bishop'. In no time the whole assembly took it up, and he was unable to refuse. He was thirty-five at the time, and was neither baptized nor ordained, but these followed immediately, and he devoted himself to the study of theology and to the writings mainly of Origen and Basil.

Ambrose was a strong and loving man, and few bishops have been more popular with ordinary people. He opposed the Arian teaching that denied the divinity of Jesus, and resolutely upheld the true faith. He kept nothing for himself and gave away his entire wealth to the poor and the Church, and also helped to build monasteries. He worked hard, lived a humble life and interceded daily for his people. It is said that when he baptized new Christians he first washed their feet, after the manner of Jesus in the Upper Room. Although extremely busy, he had time for everyone, and all sorts of people felt free to call on him. It was Ambrose who, by his powerful preaching and spiritual appeal, led the profligate Augustine back to Christianity, and what a loss this would have been to the Church otherwise.

Ambrose was a man of great courage. Milan in those days was the principal seat of the imperial government of the Western Empire. As bishop Ambrose played an active role in its politics and policies and was never slow to rebuke the secular authorities. He was a firm believer in the Church's independence, and when he thought the Emperor Valentinian was meddling in church affairs he made his famous declaration: 'The Emperor is in the Church, not over it'. He also condemned Theodosius, Emperor of the East, for his massacre of thousands of people in Thessalonica, and refused to give him the sacrament until he had made public penance.

Ambrose died on Good Friday – a worthy servant of Christ, a loving and courageous man and an example to us all, not least to church leaders who are called to serve.

Lord, teach me to seek you,
and reveal yourself to me as I seek.
For I cannot seek you unless first you teach me,
nor find you unless first you reveal yourself to me.

O Lord, who has mercy on all, take away from me my sins, and mercifully kindle in me the fire of your Holy Spirit. Take away from me the heart of stone, and give me a heart of flesh, a heart to love and adore you, a heart to delight in you, to follow and to enjoy you, for Christ's sake.

ST JEROME

c.342–420

Biblical Scholar and Translator

FEAST DAY: *30 September*

All visitors to Bethlehem are attracted to the grotto that commemorates Christ's birthplace, but many miss the adjoining cave that was home and study for several years of St Jerome, scholar and translator of the Bible.

Jerome, who was born in North Italy, was sent to Rome at the age of seventeen to finish his education. Following his baptism he travelled in France, where he renounced the secular life in favour of asceticism and scholarship. In due course he set out for Palestine, but was taken ill at Antioch as a result of his hard life. In a dream he believed God was judging him for being more interested in secular books than in the Bible, and he vowed to make Bible study his life's priority. For ten years Jerome lived as a hermit alone in the desert, intensively studying the languages of Hebrew and Greek, so that he could understand the original biblical text. Returning to Antioch, he was ordained, and after further studies he went back to Rome.

The Pope soon recognized Jerome's scholarship and made him his secretary, but Jerome jeopardized his promising career by his quarrelsome temperament. He also preached some forthright sermons against wealthy Christians, and promoted the ideal of asceticism. He returned once more to Palestine and finally settled at Bethlehem, where he founded a monastery and, in the cramped conditions of his cave, worked on what was to be his supreme accomplishment – the translation of the Bible into Latin. It became known as the Vulgate (from the Latin *vulgatus* meaning 'made known to the people'), and it was to be the standard version of the Bible in Europe for over 1,000 years.

A prayer of St Jerome reflects his love for the Bible, and it is one that we can make our own:

> O Lord, you have given us your word for a light to shine upon our path; grant us so to meditate on that word, and to follow its teaching, that we may find in it the light that shines more and more until the perfect day; through Jesus Christ our Lord.

St Jerome believed that as in prayer we speak to God, so in reading the Bible with understanding, we listen to God. Reading and prayer therefore belong together, and we move from one to the other in a dialogue with God. In this way he linked his two chief interests – Bible study and the ascetic life.

Show your mercy to me, O Lord,
and so gladden my heart.
I am like the man on the road to Jericho
who was attacked by robbers,
wounded and left for dead.
You who are the Good Samaritan, lift me up;
be kind to me according to your pleasure,
that I may dwell in your house
all the days of my life,
and praise you for ever with those who are there.

ST JOHN CHRYSOSTOM

*c.*347–407

Patriarch of Constantinople

FEAST DAY: *13 September (West) or 13 November (East)*
(formerly 27 January)

John was named Chrysostom, meaning 'golden-voice', because of his special skill at preaching. He is reputed to have been one of the Church's most accomplished preachers.

Born at Antioch in Syria, he was trained in oratory and the law, and studied theology. When he felt God was calling him to the monastic life, he became a hermit and lived in a nearby mountain cave. But the damp conditions affected his health, and he returned to Antioch where he served as deacon under Bishop Flavian. He was later ordained a priest and appointed to the special task of preaching and helping the poor of the city. He soon became famous as a preacher and expounder of the Scriptures, in which he emphasized the natural or literal meaning of the Bible (as distinct from allegorical), and its practical application.

In recognition of his skills he was consecrated Archbishop of Constantinople, a prestigious appointment which he accepted with great reluctance, due to unpleasant competition for its vacancy. Theophilus, Bishop of Alexandria, had coveted the post, and his embittered jealousy quickly made life very difficult for John.

The new Archbishop set about cleaning up the city's vices, including corruption among court officials and clergy, and his forthright sermons aimed at them invoked their wrath. He was particularly scathing of the Empress Eudoxia, whom he likened, perhaps rather tactlessly, to Jezebel! Theophilus took her side and succeeded in getting John condemned on trumped-up charges and banished to Armenia.

He returned briefly to Antioch when an earthquake convinced the frightened Eudoxia of divine retribution, but he was exiled again and died of exhaustion on the way to Cappadocia. 'Storms are all around me,' he said, 'but I fear nothing, for I stand on a rock. The turbulent sea cannot destroy the ship which is Jesus. I do not fear death nor exile, for he is everywhere – Glory to God for all things.'

St Chrysostom is an example to us of courage and faith in our witness for Christ.

O Lord, enlighten my heart, which evil desire has darkened. . . .
O Lord, help me to think of what is good.

Almighty God, who hast given us grace at this time with one accord to make our common supplications unto thee; and dost promise that when two or three are gathered together in thy Name thou wilt grant their requests: Fulfil now, O Lord, the desires and petitions of thy servants, as may be most expedient for them; granting us in this world knowledge of thy truth, and in the world to come life everlasting. *Amen.*

For the Church

O Lord our God, whose might is beyond all measure, whose wisdom beyond all understanding, whose love beyond all telling: Let thy mercies descend on us and on this house; and give to us and those who pray with us the riches of thy grace; through Jesus Christ our Saviour.

ST AUGUSTINE OF HIPPO

354–430

Bishop; Theologian

FEAST DAY: *28 August*

Augustine was born at Tagaste (in what is now Algeria) of a pagan father and Christian mother, the gentle Monica. Following a Christian upbringing he studied rhetoric at the University at Carthage, and set out for a career in philosophy. He kept a mistress for fourteen years, by whom he had a son.

Gradually his faith and desire for Christian truth diminished. He found the Scriptures 'unworthy to be compared with the dignity of Cicero', and he turned instead for spiritual and intellectual fulfilment to Manichaeism, a troublesome sect of Persian origin opposed to Christianity by its belief in dualism. (This claimed that the universe has been ruled from its creation by two conflicting powers, one good and one evil. The Bible maintained that God alone was the creator, and sustainer of all things.) But he left its ranks after nine years, finding that it created more problems about the nature of God, the world and evil than it solved. He went to Rome and founded a school of rhetoric, and later to Milan to take up a professorship.

Through all these years Augustine fought an inner battle against his sins, particularly his sensuality. In his later *Confessions* he told of storms within whirling him over the precipice of desire, enticing him even further from God. But this period of conflict was a preparation for his eventual return to faith.

The most saintly man in Milan was Bishop Ambrose, a very powerful preacher, and soon after Augustine arrived in the city he paid him a visit, not as a Christian seeking guidance, but simply because every newcomer to Milan called on Ambrose. At the same time his mother Monica came to stay with him and succeeded in persuading him to give up his mistress.

The combined influence of Ambrose and Monica helped to prepare his path to Christ. The turning point came when, in great mental turmoil, he heard what sounded like a child's voice calling, 'Take up and read.' Snatching a copy of Paul's letter to the Romans which was lying on a table, he read from Chapter 13: 'Not in rioting and drunkenness, not in strife and envy, but put ye on the Lord Jesus Christ, and make not provision for the flesh, to fulfil the lusts thereof.' 'Instantly,' he said, 'it was as if the light of peace was poured into my heart, and all the gloom and doubt vanished away.' He gladly consented to Christian baptism.

Augustine returned to Tagaste intending to found a monastery, but when he was visiting nearby Hippo in connection with this project, he was ordained to the priesthood and within four years was appointed Bishop of Hippo, remaining in that office until his death on 28 August 430.

During these years his brilliant mind never tired of turning out works on theology and philosophy. He wrote on the Trinity and the sacraments in great depth, as he did on salvation, grace, predestination and the Church. All this time he was in conflict first with the Donatists, a rigorous and schismatic sect that was troubling the Church in North Africa, and later with the Pelagian heresy. This was named after the monk, Pelagius, and rejected the doctrine of original sin and maintained that man was able to attain salvation by his own efforts and free will rather than by God's help. Augustine's attempt to stamp out Pelagianism led to the formation of his doctrine of predestination. Mankind, he believed, was tainted for ever by Adam's sin; we are saved by God's free gift of grace and not as a reward for our faith or achievements. This emphasis on God's grace became the bastion of the Reformation. Martin Luther, himself an Augustinian monk, drew his inspiration and support from the works of the great theologian, thus projecting Augustine's influence on the Church and Christian thought centuries on. He is generally regarded as the greatest Christian thinker after St Paul, and the major guardian of the true faith of the Church.

Augustine's collected writings fill fifty large volumes – a priceless gift to the Church through the centuries. At the end, when the Vandals were approaching the gates of Hippo, he produced what is ranked his greatest work – *The City of God*. Of that 'city' the elect of Christ are members. They love God, in contrast to the inhabitants of the worldly 'city' who love themselves and rebel against God. All of history is a clash between the two kingdoms, but Augustine believed that the kingdom of Christ would prevail against all the assaults of evil and be increasingly established in the world.

O thou who art the light of the minds that know thee,
  the life of the souls that love thee,
    and the strength of the wills that serve thee;
Help us so to know thee that we may truly love thee,
  so to know thee that we may fully serve thee,
    whom to serve is perfect freedom;
      through Jesus Christ our Lord.

Almighty God, in whom we live and move
and have our being, you have made us for yourself, so
that our hearts are restless until they rest in you; grant
us purity of heart and strength of purpose, that no
selfish passion may hinder us from knowing your will,
no weakness from doing it; but that in your light we
may see light clearly, and in your service find our
perfect freedom; through Jesus Christ our Lord.

Blessed are all your saints, our God and King,
who have travelled over this life's tempestuous sea and
have arrived in the harbour of peace and happiness.
Guard us who are still on our dangerous voyage, and
remember those who face storms of trouble and
temptation. Our vessel is frail, and the ocean is wide, so
steer the vessel of our life towards the eternal shore of
peace, and bring us finally to the tranquil haven of our
heart's desire, where you live and reign for ever.

ST PATRICK

c.389–c.461

Missionary to Ireland and Patron Saint

FEAST DAY: *17 March*

Patrick's birthplace in Britain is uncertain, with claims for Dumbarton on the Clyde and for Cumberland, south of Hadrian's Wall. We know that at the age of sixteen he was seized from his father's farm by Irish raiders and sold as a slave in Ireland.

During his six years of captivity he worked as a herdsman, possibly near Ballymena in County Antrim, and prayed, he said, up to a hundred prayers each day, for then, as he tells us in his autobiography, the spirit was fervent within. Eventually he escaped on a ship bound for France and in due course made his way home. All the while he dreamed of Ireland, and believed God was calling him to return as a missionary to his place of captivity. He was poorly educated, but appears to have received some training in the monastery of Lerins in France and afterwards at Auxeree, where he was ordained.

He went in 431 to assist Palladius, the first bishop of the Irish, but soon Palladius died and Patrick was consecrated bishop by St Germanus. He worked mainly in the north, at Armagh, and from there planned his evangelizing activities. He confronted King Laoghaire with the gospel, converted members of the royal household, subdued the opposing Druids, and gained freedom for Christianity. He travelled all over Ireland, founding monasteries, churches and schools. He regretted his poor scholarship, though he knew his Bible well, but what he lacked in this way he made up for in spiritual conviction and in a deep love for his people.

In his *Confessions* Patrick saw himself as a lowly servant of Christ who had called him to bring the gospel to the pagan people of Ireland. 'I am ready and willing to give my life and spend myself even to death in this country . . . I shall wait among this people for Christ's promise to gather men from the east and west to sit down with Abraham, Isaac and Jacob.' Revered by Catholics and Protestants alike, St Patrick is, in every Irish heart, a true saint.

The 'Breastplate' attributed to St Patrick is among the most familiar works of Christian devotion, and is itself a statement of faith and a true prayer.

The 'Breastplate'

> May the strength of God pilot us.
> May the power of God preserve us.
> May the wisdom of God instruct us.
> May the hand of God protect us.
> May the way of God direct us.
> May the shield of God defend us.
> May the host of God guard us
> > against the snares of evil
> > and the temptations of the world.
>
> May Christ be with us, Christ before us,
> > Christ in us, Christ over us.
>
> May thy salvation, O Lord, be always ours
> this day and for evermore. Amen.

ST BRIDGET (ST BRIDE)

c.460–c.523

Abbess of Kildare

FEAST DAY: *1 February*

Legends surround many saints, and none more than St Bridget, sometimes called St Bride, patron saint of Ireland alongside St Patrick.

It is said that as a child she gave a drink to a thirsty traveller and the water turned into milk; that the cows she owned gave milk three times a day, and that a cloak she placed on a sunbeam stayed there until the sun went down! We know that she lived in Ireland during the time of St Patrick and St Columba, that she was the daughter of a chieftain and that her mother had been a slave.

Supposedly baptized by St Patrick, Bridget soon showed remarkable spiritual awareness and decided to become a nun. She was very beautiful and had lots of offers of marriage which she refused. Her attractiveness, in fact, was a hindrance, and she prayed, 'O Lord, take away my beauty, then I can serve you alone.' At eighteen she founded a nunnery at Cill-Dara (today's Kildare). Apparently this was a 'double monastery', open to men as well as women – not an uncommon practice among the Celts – and she presided as abbess over both communities. It was Ireland's first monastery.

An early biography describes her character in glowing words – humble, gentle, prayerful, patient and forgiving; single-hearted towards God and compassionate towards the poor. Bridget was indeed generous all her life. As a young child she was sent one day to fetch butter, but on the way home she met someone who was hungry and gave it all away. She was always concerned about people's physical needs, and devoted much time to putting the teaching of God's love into practice. And she was practical in the way she ran her nunnery. Several of her monks and nuns were skilled in creating beautiful works of art and in copying and illuminating books and manuscripts.

And shining through it all was her remarkable sanctity. A bishop of the Irish Church once announced to a church gathering that he had had a vision of the Blessed Virgin Mary, and when Bridget appeared before them he cried, 'There is the holy maiden I saw in my dream'. Thereafter she came to be known as 'Mary of the Irish.' Her cult spread soon after her death, especially in Ireland and in churches abroad of Irish origin, and in Britain several churches were dedicated to her honour, most notably St Bride's in Fleet Street, London, and several in Wales. The name of St Bride's Bay in Dyfed shows the strong link between Irish and Welsh Christianity.

O God, bless my kitchen, that there may always be enough in it to give to those in need.

We implore thee, by the memory of thy cross's hallowed and most bitter anguish, make us fear thee, make us love thee, O Christ.

ST BENEDICT

c.480–c.550

'Father of Western Monasticism'; Patron
Saint of Europe

FEAST DAY: *21 March or 11 July (Roman Calendar)*

In the opinion of one modern-day churchman,
many of the problems faced by church communities
today could have been avoided if the wise 'Rule' of
Benedict had been known and followed more
closely.

As a manual of instruction in monastic living,
produced as far back as the early part of the sixth
century, Benedict's Rule has lasting value. It became the monastic code of Western Europe and enabled monasteries to become centres of learning,
hospitality, medicine and agriculture. The Rule is a
deeply spiritual work, comprehensive and full of
good sense. Within a framework of authority and
obedience, a monk, having committed his life to
Christ, was called upon to serve God and his fellow
men, and this he did through liturgical worship,
sacred reading and manual labour. Work, in fact,
was of great importance and part of the glory of life,
whereas idleness was a danger to the soul. The
writer would undoubtedly be distressed at today's
widespread unemployment!

Benedict was born at Nursia in central Italy, and
went as a student to Rome at a time when the
Empire was overrun by Barbarians and breaking
up. The moral depravity that he saw there so dis-
turbed him that he withdrew to live as a hermit in a
mountain cave at Subiaco. Others joined him and
formed small monastic communities, but jealousy

among them and an attempt on his life forced Benedict to leave.

In due course he established a monastery on the summit of Monte Cassino, near Naples. There he remained for the rest of his life and was much sought after for his miracles and prophetic gifts. He was a man whose spiritual depth and loving care endeared him to his monks and village peasants alike. It was here that he wrote his famous Rule, based on some earlier monastic teaching but so modified as to be virtually his own. Monte Cassino became the most famous monastery in Western Christendom, and the home of the Benedictine Order.

Interestingly, there is no record to say Benedict was ordained priest, nor does it seem he intended founding an order for clerics. His Rule was his chief aim and accomplishment.

This is the only prayer that has come down to us from St Benedict

O gracious and holy Father,
Give us wisdom to perceive thee,
diligence to seek thee,
patience to wait for thee,
eyes to behold thee,
a heart to meditate upon thee,
and a life to proclaim thee;
Through the power of the Spirit
of Jesus Christ our Lord.

ST COLUMBA

521–97

Abbot and Missionary

FEAST DAY: *9 June*

Columba's biographer, Adamnan, who succeeded him as Abbot of Iona, wrote of the saint:

> He had the face of an angel; was of a perfect nature, accomplished in speech, holy in deed, great in counsel. Not for a single hour did he refrain from prayer, reading or writing. He endured the rigours of fasting and vigils through night and day. But in spite of his labours he was loving to all, holy and serene, always rejoicing in the joy of the Holy Spirit.

Columba was born at County Donegal, of a noble Irish family. Following his education in several monasteries he wandered around Northern Ireland for fifteen years preaching and founding monasteries – the most notable being at Derry, Durrow and Kells.

In 536 he left Ireland for the island of Iona, off the south-west coast of Scotland. One reason for leaving, according to tradition, was his quarrel with Diarmaid, overlord of Ireland. This may be partly true, but none can doubt Columba's great love for Christ and consequent urge to preach the gospel as a missionary. This is the only motive ascribed to him by Adamnan.

Columba landed at Iona on the eve of Pentecost with twelve companions, all blood relations, and remained there for thirty-four years. The only interruptions were brief, though important, visits to his homeland and missionary travels to the Scottish mainland and neighbouring islands. He was in priest's orders only, but was recognized everywhere as the Church's chief authority. Iona became the centre of Celtic Christianity and mother to several daughter monasteries in Scotland and England. Many were converted through Columba's preaching, including Brude, King of the Picts.

As Columba was copying a verse from the Psalms, 'They that love the Lord shall lack no good thing', he suddenly stopped and ordered his cousin to complete it. He died the next day as he raised his arms in blessing on his brethren.

The Iona Community, founded in 1938 by George Macleod, is the latest development in Columba's original monastic initiative. Its members are clergy and laity of the Church of Scotland who live together at the abbey for three months in preparation for their work in Scotland's industries and her Church's mission abroad. But a visit to Iona is a spiritual experience which we who are today's Christian pilgrims ought to seek, if at all possible.

> Be thou a bright flame before me,
> Be thou a guiding star above me,
> Be thou a smooth path below me,
> Be thou a kindly shepherd behind me,
> Today – tonight – and forever.

Almighty Father, Son and Holy spirit,
eternal, blessed and gracious God,
allow me, the least of saints, to keep open a door in paradise,
the smallest and least-used door, the furthest door,
only so long as it is in your house, O God,
and I can see your glory from afar,
and hear your voice,
and know that I am with you, my God.

ST BEDE (the Venerable)

673–735

Biblical Scholar and 'Father of English History'

FEAST DAY: *27 May or 25 May (Roman Calendar)*

Bede was an Englishman, born at Wearmouth, Jarrow. From the age of seven he was educated at Wearmouth monastery and later transferred to Jarrow. He remained a member of the joint monasteries for the rest of his life. Apart from visits to York and Lindisfarne, it is unlikely he travelled beyond Northumbria.

He was ordained to the priesthood at the age of thirty, and devoted the remainder of his years to the study of the Scriptures, to teaching and writing. At one time he had 600 pupil monks.

A prodigious worker and brilliant scholar, his learning is said to have embraced all areas of contemporary knowledge and made him a teacher of generations to come. He wrote commentaries on the Scriptures and on the writings of early saints, including Augustine, Jerome, Ambrose and Gregory, as well as his own works on theology, chronology and natural phenomena.

He is remembered especially for his *Ecclesiastical History of the English Nation* completed in 731. It became the main source of information regarding the early Christianization of Britain and the English Church up to the time of his death. In it he meticulously separated historical fact from hearsay and tradition, carefully sifting every piece of evidence and listing his authorities, so that it was an invaluable help to later scholars and to all of us who prize well-founded truth. Remarkably, only in his last illness did he have any secretarial help – 'I am my own secretary: I dictate, I compose, I copy all myself.'

The title 'Venerable' was added by his religious associates less than a century after his death in recognition of his fine scholarship, and his cult as a saint has inspired many in places of learning. (On a personal note, I am pleased to record a happy association over several years with St Bede's School in Redhill, Surrey, the first joint Anglican-Roman Catholic school of its kind in Britain.)

Although a dying man, Bede insisted on completing his translation of St John's Gospel. Successful but exhausted with the effort he called his monks to him, distributed among them his few belongings, sang the Gloria, and passed to his rest. He was buried at Jarrow, but his remains were later laid to rest in Durham Cathedral.

A prayer reflecting Bede's scholarly way of life.

I ask you, good and loving Jesus, that as you graciously permitted me to drink with delight your words of
  knowledge,
so, by your mercy, you will allow me to come one day to you, the source of all wisdom, and to stand before you face to face.

> Be thou our present joy O Lord,
> Who wilt be ever our reward;
> And, as the countless ages flee,
> May all our glory be in thee.

ALCUIN

735–804

Scholar; Writer; Ecclesiastical Adviser

Alcuin was born at York and educated in its celebrated cathedral school, of which he became head. On his way home from Rome in 781 he met Charlemagne, who appointed him chief minister and adviser in religious and educational affairs.

As royal tutor living at the court, Alcuin held a prominent position. In addition to advising the King he superintended several schools in the realm. In 796 Charlemagne made him Abbot of the monastery of St Martin of Tours, famous as a great centre of learning, and he became responsible for education in the entire Frankish domain.

He was an outstanding success. From the day of his appointment to his death at Tours, Alcuin worked tirelessly in the cause of education and religion. At Tours he founded a school library, wrote several educational manuals and was a poet of repute. With the King's support he revived the study of the Classics, a discipline close to his heart, and under him biblical studies became far more attractive and beneficial. He believed Classical and ecclesiastical traditions belonged together, and that by combining them the Church became the true guardian of civilization. Under Alcuin the entire intellectual life of the state was raised to a new level. At a time when the Anglo-Saxon race was producing men of learning, he was said to be one of the finest.

Besides being an intellectual, Alcuin had an

attractive personality and ready wit, and was boyish in many ways.

His greatest agony of soul came with the invasion of the Northmen, Danish raiders who plundered abbeys and churches, killing monks and priests without mercy. Lindisfarne Abbey was gutted, church plate, jewels and vestments were stolen, and monks who had not been put to death were carried off to be sold as slaves in European markets.

Writing in great distress from Charlemagne's court, Alcuin said, 'For three hundred and fifty years we and our forefathers have dwelt in this fair land, and never before have we witnessed in Britain such terrible things as we have now suffered from the heathen.'

Alcuin's prayers mainly reflect his scholarly mind and outlook:

Grant me grace, Lord, to be strong and wise
in all things. Grant me a generous love. Fill me with
the spirit of intelligence and wisdom. Let me always be
mindful of others. O perfect and eternal Light,
enlighten me.

Good Lord, you have refreshed our souls with
the streams of knowledge; lead us at the last to
yourself, its source and spring.

And it is in his best-known prayer that this concept of spiritual enlightenment finds its noblest expression:

Eternal Light, shine into our hearts,
Eternal Goodness, deliver us from evil,
Eternal Power, be our support,
Eternal Wisdom, scatter the darkness of our ignorance,
Eternal Pity, have mercy upon us;
that with all our heart and mind and soul and strength
we may seek thy face and be brought by thine infinite
    mercy
to thy holy presence; through Jesus Christ our Lord.

Holy Lord, Almighty and Eternal Father, I give
    thanks for your mercy that has protected me
throughout this day. Let me pass this night peacefully
and with a clean mind and body that rising purely in
    the morning, I may render you grateful service.

ALFRED THE GREAT

849–901

King of Wessex

If asked what we know of King Alfred, we will probably tell the story of how he was rebuked by a village woman for burning her cakes! Behind the legend, however, is a man of true greatness – said to be the one British monarch worthy to be called 'Great'.

Alfred was born at Wantage in Berkshire, and ruled as King of Wessex for thirty years until his death. He succeeded his brother Ethelred to the throne at a critical time in the nation's history. The Danes (Northmen) were rapidly gaining ground everywhere, plundering and killing, but thanks to Alfred's long and courageous stand against them they were defeated and pushed back to the north and east of the country. The Danish King Guthrum made his peace with Alfred and was baptized a Christian.

It is claimed that from his cradle Alfred was 'filled with the love of wisdom above all things'. This scholarly king gathered many other scholars from his own country and Europe to help him translate a number of popular Latin works into Anglo-Saxon, including the *Consolations* of Boethius and the *Soliloquies* of St Augustine, and through his connexion with Rome he was able to obtain books and form libraries.

Alfred's love of learning awakened the mind of the nation, and with him came the birth of English law and literature. He founded scholarly monastic communities, saw to the education of clergy, built schools and in every way possible promoted education and culture. His enterprise was founded on a sound morality based on the Ten Commandments, and he had in his heart a deep love for Christ.

A biographer records that under Alfred, Anglo-Saxon achievement reached its finest expression, and that his age, after the darkness of the Viking night and before the coming of the Normans, was a golden interlude in our history.

In one of his own writings Alfred said 'He seems to me a very foolish man, and very wretched, who will not increase his understanding while he is in the world, and ever wish and long to reach that endless life where all shall be made clear.'

Lord God Almighty, shaper and ruler of all creatures, we pray that by your great mercy and by the token of your holy cross, you will guide us to your will and to the need of our souls. Make our minds steadfast, strengthen us against temptation, and save us from all unrighteousness. Shield us against our foes, seen and unseen. Teach us to do your will that we may inwardly love you before all things with a clean mind and a clean body. For you are our Maker and Redeemer, our help and comfort, our trust and hope, now and ever.

ST ANSELM

1033–1109

Benedictine Monk; Archbishop of Canterbury; Theologian

FEAST DAY: 21 *April*

Anselm was a native of Aosta in northern Italy, the son of a wealthy landowner. He led an undisciplined life for several years and at the age of 23 crossed the Alps into France. Three years later he entered the monastery of Bec in Normandy where he was greatly influenced by the Abbot Lanfranc, a fellow Italian. Anselm so excelled in the study of theology and philosophy that he was named Prior of the monastery and later Abbot when Lanfranc was appointed Archbishop of Canterbury.

To this period belong Anselm's remarkable personal prayers and meditations, as well as his famous metaphysical proofs of the existence and nature of God.

As Abbot of Bec he travelled to England where the abbey held property, and this enabled him to renew his friendship with Lanfranc. But very soon the Archbishop died, and the English clergy chose Anselm to succeed him. King William Rufus, however, kept the see of Canterbury vacant for four years for the sake of its revenues. During those years Anselm remained in exile in Rome, where he had gone to plead his case before the Pope.

He returned to Canterbury on the death of the King, only to encounter opposition from William's successor, Henry I, largely over the right of investiture. Anselm went again to Rome and to a further period in exile, but returned to England with the full support of the Pope.

His stand was always based on what he believed

to be God's will for the Church, and he was totally committed to the defence of the Church against worldly powers. He remained in England and died at Canterbury at the age of 76.

An outstanding scholar of the Church, who was seen as an intellectual rebel obsessed with sin and guilt, Anselm was nonetheless warm-hearted, winning the affection of all classes. He had a great love for the poor, and was one of the first to oppose the evils of the slave trade.

In his prayer of intercession we see the depth of his concern for those in need.

God of love, whose compassion never fails;
we bring to you the sufferings of all mankind;
the needs of the homeless; the cry of prisoners;
the pains of the sick and injured; the sorrow of the bereaved;
the helplessness of the aged and weak.
Strengthen and relieve them, Father,
according to their various needs and your great mercy;
for the sake of your Son our Saviour Jesus Christ.

O Lord our God,
grant us grace to desire you with our whole heart,
that so desiring you we may seek and find you,
and in finding you, may love you,
and in loving you, may hate those sins
from which you have redeemed us.

O merciful God, fill our hearts, we pray, with the graces of your Holy Spirit; with love, joy, peace, patience, gentleness, goodness, faithfulness, humility and self-control,
Teach us to love those who hate us; to pray for those who despitefully use us; that we may be the children of your love, our Father, who makes the sun to rise on the evil and the good, and sends rain on the just and on the unjust.

ST FRANCIS OF ASSISI

1181–1226

Founder of the Franciscan Order

FEAST DAY: *4 October*

We attribute to Francis of Assisi one of the loveliest
and most familiar of prayers:

> Lord, make us instruments of thy peace; where
> there is hatred, let us sow love; where there is in-
> jury, pardon; where there is discord, union; where
> there is doubt, faith; where there is despair, hope;
> where there is darkness, light; where there is sad-
> ness, joy; for thy mercy and for thy truth's sake. O
> divine Master, grant that we may not so much seek
> to be consoled as to console; to be understood as to
> understand; to be loved, as to love; for it is in giving
> that we receive; it is in pardoning that we are par-
> doned; it is in dying that we are born to eternal life.

Francis was born in the town of Assisi in Central
Italy. He was named Giovanni, but was always
known by his nickname Francis. He was a mis-
chievous youth, but following an illness his thoughts
and behaviour turned to more serious things, and he
began to spend time in prayer and meditation and to
give money to the poor. While on a pilgrimage to
Rome he was deeply moved at the sight of beggars
around St Peter's, and exchanging clothes with one
of them, he became a beggar for a day.

Back in Assisi, where his wealthy father
now disowned him, he one day met a leper. His
first reaction was to keep his distance, but the fact
that Jesus had touched a leper came as a piercing
and compelling challenge. Kneeling beside the

stricken man, he kissed him and gave him money.

In a church service Francis heard Jesus' call to his disciples: 'Heal the sick, raise the dead, cleanse lepers, cast out devils. You received without cost; give without charge.' He knew then he was being called to become a wandering preacher, owning nothing and begging for food and shelter.

He went about barefooted, wearing a rough woollen tunic, and spent his time among the poor and sick. He owned nothing, in stark contrast to his earlier life, but he had never been happier. Through the day he would sing his canticles ('little songs'), preach to the villagers and even to the birds, for he had a close affinity with nature.

Francis attracted followers for whom he drafted a Rule composed of the commands of Jesus, in particular, 'Love one another'. The Pope gave his blessing to the new movement, called at first the 'Friars Minor' or 'Lesser Brothers'. They followed Francis' example in preaching and caring for lepers and outcasts, and each friar learned a trade so that they resorted to begging only when it was unavoidable.

Following Francis' death at the early age of forty-five, his monastic movement known as 'Franciscans' spread throughout Europe, producing many fine scholars and devout followers over the years. The town of Assisi and the shrine of St Francis continue to attract many tourists and pilgrims.

In a world of much discord and sadness we need to pray and live Francis' prayer for peace, love, pardon, faith, hope, light and joy.

God Almighty, Eternal, Righteous, and Merciful, give to us poor sinners to do for thy sake all that we know of thy will, and to will always what pleases thee, so that inwardly purified, enlightened, and kindled by the fire of the Holy Spirit, we may follow in the footprints of thy well-beloved Son, our Lord Jesus Christ.

Be thou praised, O Lord, for those who
forgive for love of thee, and bear sufferings and
tribulations. Blessed are they who are steadfast in peace,
for by thee, Most High, shall they be crowned.

ST BERNARD OF CLAIRVAUX

1090–1153

Cistercian Monk and Abbot

FEAST DAY: *20 August*

For a combination of hard work and spiritual devotion, we could hardly find a better example than Bernard of Clairvaux.

Born at Fontaines in Burgundy, of wealthy parents, Bernard was expected to become a soldier-knight like his father, but his mother hoped he would choose the monastic life. She died when he was young, but her wish was fulfilled. Praying alone one day in a little chapel in the woods, he claimed to hear Jesus say to him, 'Come to me . . . and I will give you rest' and soon he felt at peace. At the age of twenty-two and with several companions he entered the monastery of Citeaux. The rules were strict, but Bernard's dedication impressed everyone, and resulted in an influx of new recruits, thereby saving the monastery from closure. It marked also the turning-point in the history of western monasticism.

When the monastery became overcrowded the Abbot ordered that Bernard should leave with a group of twelve monks and establish a daughter monastery elsewhere. They chose a place in the Champagne region called the 'Valley of Wormwood', which Bernard renamed 'Clairvaux' – 'Valley of Light' – 'for from it the Gospel will spread far and wide,' he said.

The monks laboured tirelessly for long hours, building their house and preparing the barren soil for crops. But their efforts were rewarded as the monastery prospered to become one of the major centres of the Cistercian Order. During the lifetime of Bernard, its celebrated Abbot, a number of monasteries were founded, including Waverley in Surrey, Rievaulx and Fountains in Yorkshire, and Tintern in Gwent, and at the time of his death there were about 500 houses throughout Europe, fifty of them in England and Wales.

Bernard had become so popular and respected that even Kings and Popes sought his counsel. He became known as 'the conscience of the Christian World', and later, Martin Luther described him as 'greater than all other monks and priests throughout the globe'. But Bernard was humble and never wanted fame. He was sometimes involved in controversy and made enemies as well as friends, but nothing hindered his devotion to Christ.

Among Bernard's sayings there is one that is particularly well known: 'Take away free will and there is nothing left to be saved: take away grace and there is no means left of saving. Salvation is accomplished when both co-operate.' And he left us one of the loveliest hymns of Christian devotion, which we could well use as a regular prayer:

Jesus, the very thought of Thee
With sweetness fills the breast;
But sweeter far Thy face to see,
And in Thy presence rest.

O God, whose greatness knows no limits,
whose wisdom no bounds, whose peace excels all understanding; you who love and help us beyond measure – help us to love you. Though we cannot fully do so because of your infinite goodness, increase and deepen our understanding so that we may love you more and more; through Jesus Christ our Lord.

ST CLARE OF ASSISI

1194–1253

Founder of the 'Poor Clares'

FEAST DAY: *11 (formerly 12) August*

On Palm Sunday in the year 1212, a young woman
of eighteen was worshipping in the Cathedral of
Assisi. She was too shy to make her way to the altar
where the bishop was blessing and distributing
palms, but he had noticed her, and kindly went to
where she stood. Taking the palm in her trembling
hand, she felt a direct call from God to a life of
Christian obedience and service.

She was Clare Offreduccio, daughter of wealthy
parents. That evening she ran away from home to
the nearby town and church of Portiuncula, where
St Francis of Assisi lived with his religious community. Gaining admittance she discarded her fine
clothes, allowed her hair to be cut, and put on the
coarse penitential habit of the Franciscans. Francis
had not yet founded a women's convent, so Clare
was sent to one run by Benedictine nuns not far
away. Later, Francis allowed her to use the Church
of St Damiano in Assisi, where he himself had
heard God's call, and from there she established her
own religious community. In time other members
of her family, including her sister and her mother,
joined her.

Clare's Rule was one of strictest poverty, and her
nuns were known as 'Poor Clares'. They possessed
nothing of their own. They wore neither shoes nor
stockings, never ate meat, slept on the floor and
relied almost entirely on alms. Clare was even more
ascetic than her nuns; she wore a hair shirt and took

nothing but bread and water during Lent. In spite of pressures to have her relax the Rule demanding absolute poverty, she resisted. She once said: 'They say we are too poor. Can a heart which possesses God really be called poor?'

But for all the strictness of her Order, Clare was cheerful and kind. She enjoyed music and, like St Francis, loved nature in all its variety and splendour. She is said to have thanked God constantly for the glory of life and to have wept at the thought of Christ's Passion, and she welcomed the chance to bathe the feet of a leper.

Clare patiently suffered years of sickness. When she lay dying she was twice visited by the Pope, who gave her absolution. Once she was heard to say: 'Depart in peace, for the road thou hast followed is the good one.' When asked to whom she was speaking, she replied, 'I am speaking to my departing soul, and he who was its guide is not far away.'

I pray you, O most gentle Jesus, having redeemed me by baptism from original sin, so now by your Precious Blood, which is offered and received throughout the world, deliver me from all evils, past, present and to come. By your most cruel death give me lively faith, a firm hope and perfect charity, so that I may love you with all my heart and all my soul and all my strength. Make me firm and steadfast in good works and grant me perseverance in your service so that I may be able to please you always.

ST RICHARD OF CHICHESTER

1197–1253

Bishop of Chichester

FEAST DAY: 3 *April*

Richard was born at Wyche (the present Droitwich) in Worcestershire, the son of a farmer. He was a studious boy and determined from an early age to follow an academic career. On his parents' death, however, the assets left to Richard and his brother were mishandled by a negligent guardian, and the boys were soon penniless. Without hesitation Richard gave up his studies and tirelessly helped his brother to save the family farm.

Richard eventually returned to his books. He studied at Oxford, Paris and Bologna and gained a reputation as a scholar. Edmund, the Archbishop of Canterbury, chose Richard as his Chancellor, and he then shared the burden of his Archbishop's struggle against King Henry III who would either keep benefices vacant so as to reap their revenues or fill them with unsuitable favourites of his own. Richard remained faithful to his Archbishop and accompanied him in exile. When Edmund died, exhausted by troubles, Richard was heartbroken and entered a monastery.

Following his ordination he became parish priest at Deal in Kent, performing his duties, it is said, like the poor priest in the Canterbury Tales 'rich in holy thought and work, preaching the gospel gladly and teaching the flock devoutly'. But being a man of outstanding ability he was destined for more notable service, and was recalled by the new Archbishop to his former chancellorship. When the

Bishop of Chichester died in 1244 Richard was appointed to succeed him.

The King bitterly opposed the appointment and tried, unsuccessfully, to get a man of his choice elected. Although the doors of his cathedral were barred against him, Richard wasted no time in getting to know the clergy and people of his diocese. During this period of exile he was completely dependent on the charity and hospitality of others, but everyone grew to love him for his kindly ways and deeds of compassion.

At last the Pope ordered the King to give in under threat of excommunication, and Richard took possession of Chichester Cathedral. On the day of his enthronement thousands lined the route and joined in the celebrations. He was Bishop for only eight years, but during that time he endeared himself to all.

Responding to the Pope's request to lead a crusade for the recovery of the Holy Land, he set off, but the journey proved too much, and he died at Dover in a house for poor priests and pilgrims.

The prayer of St Richard as he lay dying

Thanks be to thee, my Lord Jesus Christ,
 For all the benefits thou hast won for me,
 For all the pains and insults thou hast borne for me.
O most merciful Redeemer, Friend and Brother,
 May I know thee more clearly,
 Love thee more dearly,
 And follow thee more nearly;
  For ever and ever. *Amen.*

ST BONAVENTURE

1221–74

Franciscan Theologian

FEAST DAY: *15 July*

Bonaventure, who was born in Italy, became a Franciscan when he was twenty-two. He was a brilliant student of theology at Paris University, and remained there as a lecturer. At thirty-six he was elected Minister General of the Franciscan Order, and was regarded as its second founder, after St Francis. He spent much of his time sorting out internal disputes that had weakened the Order. He wrote a biography of St Francis, and called for a greater observance of rules and intellectual discipline.

On a visit to England Bonaventure was offered the archbishopric of York, but declined. Soon afterwards he became a Cardinal and was appointed Bishop of Albano. When the papal envoys brought news of his appointment he was washing dishes in the monastery kitchen and refused to see them until he had finished. Although a brilliant scholar, he enjoyed doing ordinary jobs: 'One becomes holy,' he said, 'only by doing common things well and being constantly faithful in small things.'

We are indebted to Bonaventure for his theological writings and insights into the Church's thought of his day. He was a contemporary of St Thomas Aquinas, but whereas Aquinas held to the new Aristotelian doctrines, Bonaventure was much more in line with St Augustine. The cross of Christ was central in his life and prayer. He thought of the spiritual life as a journey of the soul into God:

through prayer we receive God's grace; by a life of virtue we become righteous; meditation leads to knowledge, and contemplation brings us wisdom. He believed we have not only bodily but spiritual senses in which the soul hears, sees, touches, smells and tastes the sweetness of God. Intelligence, simplicity and self-denial were the hallmarks of his life.

St Bonaventure wrote a hymn on our Lord's passion, which we can use in our meditation on the cross:

> Thorns and cross and nails and lance,
> Wounds, our rich inheritance. . .
> May these all our spirits fill,
> And with love's devotion thrill. . .
> Christ, by coward hands betrayed,
> Christ, for us a captive made,
> Christ, upon the bitter tree,
> Slain for man – all praise to thee.

Lord Jesus Christ, pierce my soul with your love so that I may always long for you alone, who are the bread of angels and the fulfilment of the soul's deepest desires. May my heart always hunger and feed upon you, so that my soul may be filled with the sweetness of your presence. May my soul thirst for you, who are the source of life, wisdom, knowledge, light and all the riches of God our Father. May I always seek and find you, think upon you, speak to you and do all things for the honour and glory of your holy name. Be always my only hope, my peace, my refuge and my help in whom my heart is rooted so that I may never be separated from you.

ST THOMAS AQUINAS

1225–74

Medieval Scholar and Man of Prayer

FEAST DAY: *28 January*

Thomas was born of a noble Italian family and educated at the prestigious Benedictine monastery of Monte Cassino. When he was in his mid-teens he told his family he intended entering the newly formed Dominican Order; they objected on the grounds that this was a mendicant or 'begging' Order, and Thomas was confined to the family castle for almost two years.

But his persistence won. He became a Dominican friar at nineteen and studied under the renowned St Albert the Great. Albert prophesied that the voice of the man nicknamed 'the dumb ox' because of his portly figure and silence at theological discussions, would soon be heard everywhere.

Following his ordination to the priesthood, Thomas spent the rest of his life travelling in Paris and throughout Italy, lecturing, studying and writing.

His absorbing passion was theology, to which he applied his knowledge of philosphy and logic. Popes, kings and scholars sought his wisdom. He had intense powers of concentration, and reputedly was able to dictate to four secretaries at once! At the age of forty-one he began work on his famous *Summa Theologica*, the greatest of all his written works, consisting of five large volumes of deep thought about God, our relationship to God, and Christ as our way to him.

Thomas was a humble, unassuming man. After one deep spiritual experience in prayer he suddenly felt all his writings to be 'so much straw', and he never wrote again, leaving even the *Summa* unfinished.

Scholarship and prayer were the hallmarks of his life, and he has been described as 'the most saintly of the learned and most learned of the saints'. We see in his daily prayer a feature of his scholarly devotion:

Enable me, O merciful God,
wisely to study, rightly to understand,
and perfectly to fulfil that which is pleasing to thee,
to the praise and glory of thy name.

One day near the end of his life, as he knelt before a crucifix, he heard Jesus say, 'Thomas, you have written well, what reward do you wish?' He replied, 'Nothing but yourself, Lord.'

He died, aged forty-nine, on his way to the General Council at Lyons.

Most loving Lord God, grant to me a steadfast heart which no unworthy desire may drag downwards; an unconquered heart which no hardship may wear out; an upright heart which no worthless purpose may ensnare. Impart to me also, O Lord my God, understanding to know you, diligence to seek you, a way of life to please you, and, finally, a faithfulness that may embrace you; through Jesus Christ, my Lord.

A prayer at the Sacrament

O God, who in this wondrous Sacrament has left unto us a memorial of your passion; grant us so to venerate the sacred mysteries of your body and blood, that we may ever continue to feel within ourselves the blessed fruit of your redemption; who lives and reigns one God, for ever.

ST GERTRUDE THE GREAT

1256–c.1302

German Mystic

FEAST DAY: *16 November*

Among the women who have contributed greatly to the spiritual life of the Church is St Gertrude, a Benedictine nun known as 'The Great Gertrude', to distinguish her from others of that name.

Gertrude was born at Thuringen, a region of Central Germany, and at the age of five was entrusted to a Cistercian abbey, where she was cared for and educated, and there she stayed for the rest of her life. At twenty-five she underwent various mystical experiences. Many of her visions took place during the singing of the Divine Office. As a result, she gave up studying philosophy and turned to a study of the Scriptures and the Church Fathers, continuing her work right up until her death.

Religious mystics usually have a profound sense of God's presence and a penetrating insight into some aspect of his character. For Gertrude it was God's utter self-giving which moved her to the depths of gratitude and humility. 'Lord,' she cried, 'surely the greatest of thy miracles is to compel the earth to bear such a sinner as I am.'

Gertrude likened God to a pure flame of love within the heart; everything around was illumined by the Divine Light and all of nature was sacramental – an outward sign of God's grace. All this she thought of as 'The Sacred Heart', and she is believed to be the advocate of the deep spiritual devotion bearing that name which later became popular.

One of Gertrude's prayers shows us her own heart of love and deep devotion:

O God, worthy of an infinite love,
I have nothing which can adequately measure
    your dignity,
but such is my desire towards you,
that if I had all that you have,
I would gladly and thankfully give all to you.

St Gertrude wrote of her spiritual experiences in a book called *The Herald of Divine Love*. Other writings are associated with her and her thoughts became well known once her work was translated into Latin. We have come to regard her as one of the most important of medieval mystics.

We could easily believe that mystics are all starry-eyed visionaries. But many, like Gertrude, are also known for their good works, and we need the example of both. True religion is a balance of contemplation and action, of prayer and work – the balance we find to perfection in the life and teaching of Jesus, in which prayer and care are intertwined.

O Love, O God, who created me, in your love re-create me.

O Love, who redeemed me, fill up and redeem for yourself in me whatever part of your love has fallen into neglect within me.

O Love, O God, who, to make me yours, in the blood of your Christ purchased me, in your truth sanctify me.

O Love, O God, who adopted me as a daughter, after your own heart fashion and foster me.

O Love, who as yours and not another's chose me, grant that I may cleave to you with my whole being.

O Love, O God, who first loved me, grant that with my whole heart, and with my whole soul, and with my whole strength, I may love you.

O Love, O God almighty, in your love confirm me.
O Love most wise, give me wisdom in the love of you.
O Love most sweet, give me sweetness in the taste of you.
O Love most dear, grant that I may live for you alone.
O Love most faithful, in all my tribulations comfort and succour me.
O Love who is ever with me, work all my works in me.
O Love most victorious, grant that I may persevere to the end in you.

JULIAN OF NORWICH

*c.*1342–after 1413

English Mystic

Today the East Anglian city of Norwich is busy
with people and noisy with traffic. Its population in
the late fourteenth and early fifteenth centuries was
considerably smaller, but a concentration of city
dwellers and numerous traders surrounding the
church of St Julian meant a constant din, unhelpful,
one imagines, to the contemplative life of an
anchoress living in a cell within its walls. She was
Mother Julian, the most popular and beloved of
English mystics, who probably took her name from
that of the church.

Norwich then was suffering a series of major
troubles – the Black Death, the Lollard suppression,
the Hundred Years' War and the Peasants' Revolt –
which reduced the population to one third of its
normal size. But neither din nor tragedy could
destroy her inner peace and resolute faith in God:
'All shall be well, and all shall be well, and all
manner of thing shall be well.'

Julian might well have been lost to history but
that on 8 May 1373, following a serious illness, she
received in a state of ecstacy fifteen revelations lasting five hours, and another the day after. They were
mainly visions of Christ's passion and of the Holy
Trinity. Twenty years later she wrote of her experience in *The Sixteen Revelations of Divine Love*, a work
that became a spiritual classic.

In one of her visions Julian held a hazelnut in the
palm of her hand. As she marvelled at its smallness

and very existence, she was told, 'It exists, both now and forever, because God loves it.' In short, everything owed its existence to God's love, and God in his infinite mercy is at work in his world.

In the divine and merciful love of God, believed Mother Julian, lies the clue to all mysteries and the answer to all problems. Love unites us to God and to each other. He does not coerce us, for his love is unprotected love, and in that love he forgives us. Love for others is a sign of Christ's indwelling. The work of the Holy Trinity is creative, redemptive and enabling. God is Mother as well as Father, for of him we are always being born. Prayer joins the soul to God and makes it one with his will through the inner working of the Holy Spirit. Our prayers await us in heaven and will be part of our delight. Our greatest blessing is to know God in the clearness of eternal light, 'seeing him truly, experiencing him tenderly, possessing him completely in the fulness of joy.'

A restored church stands today on the site of old St Julian's which was bombed in 1942, and attached to it is a chapel believed to be on the site of Mother Julian's cell, thus commemorating her life there and the priceless treasure of her meditations.

God, of your goodness, give me yourself, for you are sufficient for me. I cannot properly ask anything less, to be worthy of you. If I were to ask less, I should always be in want. In you alone do I have all.

Lord, you know what I want, if it be your will that I have it, and if it be not your will, good Lord, do not be displeased, for I want nothing which you do not want.

ST CATHERINE OF SIENA

1347–80

Dominican Mystic, Patron Saint of Italy and Italian Nurses

FEAST DAY: *29 April (formerly 30 April)*

Catherine showed an interest in religion from an early age, when she began devoting herself to prayer and penance. As a child she would kneel on each step of the stairs in her home and say a prayer. She was only six when she had a vision of Christ in glory amongst his apostles.

Her parents were troubled at this and tried to discourage her. Later, she refused to marry like her sisters and cut off her flowing hair to make herself unattractive to men. Her parents put her to work in the kitchen, hoping this would bring her to her senses, but when nothing daunted Catherine's determination they reluctantly allowed her to enter a Dominican convent.

She at once devoted herself to nursing the sick in a Siena hospital, choosing to care for advanced leprosy patients and those terminally ill with cancer whom others found it too difficult to tend. In a vision she heard Jesus say, 'I draw closer to you through your love for others.' Her helpers grew, among them Dominicans and Augustinians, both men and women, and they travelled with her on frequent journeys, caring for the sick and preaching the gospel. When a plague broke out in Siena Catherine moved amongst the stricken, nursing the sick, comforting the dying and bereaved, even digging graves and burying the bodies herself. Her reputation grew and she became one of the most influential spiritual leaders of the late Middle Ages, consulted for her

wisdom, holiness and good works in cities beyond
Siena. Unable to write herself, she dictated several
works of spiritual and doctrinal value.

Her later years were spent trying to heal the
internal divisions within the Church when rival
Popes in Rome and Avignon brought about the
Great Schism. But Catherine never let any pressure
distract her from communion with her Lord and
from service to the sick and poor.

Exhausted by constant work, she suffered a
paralysing stroke and died aged thirty-three.

At one period of severe trial Catherine prayed, 'O
my Saviour, my Lord, why did you leave me when I
was sorely tried?' Jesus replied, 'My child, I have been
with you all along, I was in your heart throughout.'

It is reassuring for us to know that saints, such as
Catherine, went through periods of doubt in their
journey of faith and devotion.

Eternal Trinity, you are a deep sea,
into which the more I enter the more I find,
and the more I find the more I seek.
The soul ever hungers in your abyss, Eternal Trinity,
longing to see you with the light of your light,
and as the deer yearns for the springs of water,
 so my soul yearns to leave the dark prison of this body,
and see you in truth.
Eternal Godhead, O sea profound,
what more could you give me than yourself?
You are the fire that never burns out;
You consume in your heat all the soul's self-love;
You are the flame that drives away the cold.
Give me your light that I may know all truth,
clothe me with yourself, eternal truth,
that I may live this mortal life with true obedience,
and in the light of your most holy faith.

THOMAS À KEMPIS

1380–1471

Monk and Writer

Thomas à Kempis was born Thomas Hemerken at
Kempen, near Cologne, of poor parents. He was
educated in and greatly influenced by the 'Congregation of the Common Life', an informal monastic community. In his early twenties he entered an
Augustinian monastery near Zwolle in Holland,
which his brother John had helped to establish, and
there he remained for the greater part of his life,
preaching, writing and copying manuscripts.

Little else is known of his personal life, but we are
told he was simple in worldly affairs and shy and
retiring in his ways. He was much in demand in the
monastery for his spiritual counselling, otherwise
he liked to be alone, and when conversation grew
too lively he would retire, as he put it, 'to a nook
with a book'. He was certainly a man of keen intellectual ability, with the mind of a mystic. His writings were extensive, consisting of sermons, ascetic
meditations, prayers, hymns and poems. It was,
however, as the reputed author of the book *The
Imitation of Christ* that he became famous.

Though written in a monastery, the book has
always been found relevant to Christian spirituality
in the world, and has been as popular with the laity
as with the clergy. In George Eliot's *Mill on the Floss*
Maggie Tulliver exults in it as 'a lasting record of
human needs and human consolations'.

Thomas à Kempis himself wrote, 'The whole life
of Christ was a cross and a martyrdom,' and he saw

the Christian as one who journeyed along 'the royal road of the holy cross'. He was keen to point out that the imitation of Christ did not rest only on the historical figure who lived in Palestine, died and rose again. He believed that Christ was alive for all the world, influencing and supporting men and women in their day to live his kind of life.

Thomas à Kempis gave us one of the great prayers of Christian devotion:

> Grant us, O Lord, to know that which is worth knowing, to love that which is worth loving, to praise that which can bear with praise, to hate what in thy sight is unworthy, to prize what to thee is precious, and, above all, to search out and to do what is well-pleasing unto thee; through Jesus Christ our Lord.

The prayer in itself is a call to imitate Christ, though in no way does 'imitation' mean impersonation or emulation. The person and work of Christ are unique, and no one takes his place; but we all may be 'as Christ' in the world, bearing his likeness and drawing others to him.

Lord, above all. . .
Grant me, most sweet and loving Jesus, to rest in thee
above every creature,
above all health and beauty,
above all glory and esteem,
above all power and grandeur,
above all skill and shrewdness,
above all riches and talents,
above all gladness and loftiness,
above all fame and praise,
above all hope and promise,
above all merit and desire,

above all gifts that you may shower upon me,
above all joy or jubilation that my mind may have or feel;
and, still more, above Angels and Archangels,
above all heavenly host,
above all things visible and invisible,
and above all things that you, my God, are not,
For you, my God, are best above all.

Lord, I come. . .

My God, I come to you, putting my
confidence in your mercy and generosity. I long to come
unto my Saviour; hungry and thirsty unto the fountain
of life; poor and needy unto the King of Heaven; the
servant unto his Lord, the creature unto his Maker, the
desolate to his Comforter.

ERASMUS

*c.*1466–1536

Dutch Scholar and Reformer

After an unhappy childhood and a reluctant stay in an Augustinian monastery, Desiderius Erasmus eventually found contentment and stimulus through opportunities to study and teach in France, England, Italy and Belgium. He was a brilliant scholar with particular knowledge of the Classics and the Church Fathers.

On his first visit to England he met Thomas More, the Lord Chancellor, and John Colet, who was then Dean of St Paul's, and the three formed a close friendship. It was for St Paul's School that Erasmus wrote a special prayer:

> Hear our prayers, O Lord Jesus Christ, the everlasting Wisdom of the Father. You give us in the days of our youth, aptness to learn; add, we pray, the furtherance of your grace, so to learn knowledge and the liberal sciences that, by their help, we may attain to a fuller knowledge of you, whom to know is the height of blessedness; and by the example of your boyhood, may duly increase in age, wisdom and favour with God and man.

Both Oxford and Cambridge conferred degrees on him, and at Cambridge he became Professor of Greek and Theology. In 1516 he brought out his celebrated edition of the Greek New Testament with his new translation into Classical Latin – a work that was to have an immense influence on theological studies.

Erasmus wrote a number of other works and edited the writings of the Fathers. Also from his pen came satirical works exposing the corruptions of the Church, and through these he aligned himself with his famous contemporary Martin Luther and helped to pave the way for the Reformation. But while agreeing with Luther in his condemnation of Indulgences and superstitious worship to the neglect of the teachings of the Bible, he was unable to go all the way with him. He thought Luther too extreme and devisive, whereas he himself favoured reasonableness and reconciliation. His compromise put him in a lasting dilemma, for he incurred the enmity of Catholics by not wholly disapproving of Luther, and the hatred of Protestants by not altogether supporting him, and his writings were censured and forbidden by both. Sadly, he lived to see bitterness between Catholics and Protestants spill over into persecution, and for a man of a peaceable nature this was a terrible hurt.

Much of Erasmus' later life, following his travels, was spent in Basle in Switzerland, where he was able to write and see his works published. And there he died, without the ministrations of a priest, but invoking the mercy and love of Christ.

O Lord Jesus Christ, who hast said that thou art the Way, the Truth and the Life; we pray thee, suffer us not at any time to stray from thee, who art the Way; nor to distrust thy promises, who art the Truth; nor to rest in any other thing than thee, who art the Life; beyond which there is nothing to be desired; for thou hast taught us what to believe, what to do, what to hope, and wherein to take our rest.

ST THOMAS MORE

1487–1535

Lord Chancellor of England; Martyr

FEAST DAY: *9 July*

The popular film and play of the 1960s, *A Man for All Seasons*, movingly portrayed the brilliant life and courageous death of St Thomas More, one of England's finest saints.

Thomas More showed an early interest in the Classics, but his father persuaded him to study law and he was called to the bar. He married and enjoyed a happy family life with his four children; his home in Chelsea was frequently the meeting-place for prominent scholars and churchmen, including John Colet and Erasmus. Throughout his life he recited the Little Office daily. He wore a hair shirt next to his skin and privately followed the monastic discipline.

Thomas More came to prominence with the accession to the throne of Henry VIII, who quickly recognized his qualities. His appointments under Henry included Under-Sheriff of London, Envoy to Flanders, Privy Councillor and Master of Requests, Speaker of the House of Commons, High Steward of the Universities of Oxford and Cambridge, Chancellor of the Duchy of Lancaster, and Lord Chancellor in succession to Cardinal Wolsey. He was knighted in 1521. At Flanders he wrote his famous *Utopia*, a political treatise portraying an ideal society based on reason and nature. In contrast to the poverty and squalor suffered by many, his 'commonwealth' would be based on justice and equality for all, with religious toleration and free education for both men and women. He wrote controversially of clerical abuses, and of the superstitious veneration of saints.

The turning point in his illustrious career came when he refused to support the King over his proposed divorce from Catherine of Aragon, and again when Henry wanted to be recognized as 'Protector and Supreme Head of the Church of England'. More resigned as Chancellor when he realized the King's true intentions, and as a result suffered a serious loss of income. The Act of Succession brought about the final crisis. Henry married Anne Boleyn, who was crowned Queen, but More refused to attend her coronation. And when he declined to take the oath required by the Act he was despatched to the Tower, along with Bishop John Fisher.

During his fifteen months' imprisonment More wrote devotional books and spent much time in prayer and penance. Attempts were made to induce him to conform, but in vain. For his opposition to the Act of Supremacy he was charged with high treason and beheaded on Tower Hill on 6 July 1535, after uttering his final declaration that he died for the faith of the Holy Catholic Church and was 'the King's good servant, but God's first'.

Prayers of St Thomas More after he was condemned to death

Glorious God, give me grace to amend my life and to have an eye to my end without grudge of death, which to those who die in thee, good Lord, is the gate to a wealthy life. And give me, good Lord, a humble, lowly, quiet, peaceable, patient, charitable, kind, tender and pitiful mind, in all my works and all my words and all my thoughts, to have a taste of thy holy, blessed Spirit.

Give me, good Lord, a full faith, a firm hope, and a fervent charity, a love to thee incomparably above the love of myself.

Give me thy grace, good Lord, to make death no stranger to me. Lord, give me patience in tribulation and grace in everything to conform my will to thine.

Give me, good Lord, a longing to be with thee, not to avoid the calamities of this wretched world, nor so much for the attaining of the joys of heaven, as for a true love of thee.

And give me, good Lord, thy love and favour, which my love of thee, however great, could not deserve, were it not for thy great goodness.

These things, good Lord, that I pray for, give me thy grace also to labour for.

MARTIN LUTHER

1483–1546

German Church Reformer

We can safely place Martin Luther among the select few whose views and actions changed the course of world history. In his case biblical scholarship and a profound religious experience led him to a deeper understanding of God, and subsequently brought him into conflict with the Church's authorities. This resulted in the sixteenth-century Reformation and the birth of Protestantism.

At twenty-two Luther entered the German Augustinian monastery at Erfurt in fulfilment of a vow made during a thunderstorm. He was ordained priest, and went as lecturer in moral philosophy to the newly formed Wittenberg University. Affairs of his Order took him to Rome, and on returning to Wittenberg he was made a Doctor of Theology, a Professor of Scripture, and later, Vicar of his Order, which gave him charge of a number of Augustinian monasteries.

Several factors began to impinge upon his teaching and beliefs. The religious routine failed to give him spiritual satisfaction, and he started to question the Church's doctrines and ceremonial. His own emotional and melancholy nature caused him deep anxiety about personal sin and salvation, and his reading of the Scriptures, in particular Romans, and the works of Augustine convinced him of the rightness of justification by faith rather than works: we find salvation, he believed, by personal faith in Christ and not through doing good or through the mediation of the Church and its priests.

Open conflict ensued with the sale of Indulgences – a practice authorized by Pope Leo X to raise money for the renovation of St Peter's in Rome. Luther rebelled by nailing his famous 'Ninety-Five Theses' to the door of the castle church at Wittenberg, and within a few days Germany was fermenting with the news. Martin Luther found he had support from others who wished to see the Church reformed.

At first the authorities aimed to settle the dispute by way of monastic discipline. Luther was summoned to a hearing at Heidelberg, and then tried in Rome on a charge of spreading heresy, but he refused to recant. He returned to Wittenberg under guard, and began his writings in which he went further still in his rebellion, calling on others to take up the fight. His writings were condemned; he replied by burning the papal edict, and the Church retaliated by excommunicating him. Summoned before an assembly at Worms, he supposedly uttered his famous 'Here I stand; I can do no other; God help me. Amen.' He was put under ban of the Empire.

During the next eight months at Eisenach, Luther fought off agonizing doubts about his actions. The consequences were more alarming than ever he imagined, and he felt plagued by the devil, but with God's help he won through. He married a former Cistercian nun by whom he had several children. He wrote extensively, developing his views, and not the least of his contributions was his translation of the Latin Bible into German, an invaluable gift to the Church in Germany and one that helped to form the modern German language.

In the following prayer we feel something of Martin Luther's inner struggle and utter dependence upon God:

Do thou, my God, stand by me against all the world's wisdom and reason. Thou must do it. Not mine, but thine is the cause. For my own self I have nothing to do with these great and earthly lords. I would prefer to have peaceful days, and to be out of this turmoil. But thine, O Lord, is this cause; it is righteous and eternal. Stand by me, thou true eternal God! In no man do I trust . . . Hast thou chosen me for this work? I ask thee how I may be sure of this, if it be thy will; for I would never have thought, in all my life, of undertaking aught against such great lords. Stand by me, O God, in the name of thy dear Son, Jesus Christ, who shall be my Defence and Shelter, yea, my Mighty Fortress, through the might and strength of thy Holy Spirit. God help me. Amen.

Behold, Lord, an empty vessel that needs to be filled. My Lord, fill it. I am weak in the faith; strengthen me. I am cold in love; warm me and make me fervent, that my love may go out to my neighbour. I do not have a strong and firm faith; at times I doubt and am unable to trust you altogether. O Lord, help me. Strengthen my faith and trust in you.

THOMAS CRANMER

1489–1556

Archbishop of Canterbury; Martyr

Grant, we beseech thee, merciful Lord, to thy faithful people pardon and peace; that they may be cleansed from all their sins, and serve thee with a quiet mind; through Jesus Christ our Lord. Amen.

This prayer, treasured by Christians for nearly 500 years, is one among many from the *Book of Common Prayer*, much of which is the priceless work of Thomas Cranmer.

Cranmer was a man of great learning, with a private library larger than that of Cambridge University. He was educated at Cambridge where he became a Fellow, and was later ordained to the priesthood. He had a great regard for the Bible and ordered that an English translation should be placed in every church and read aloud regularly. At the same time he was concerned about the proliferation of service books, all written in Latin, and believed the Church needed one book in English that everyone could use. Night after night his candle could be seen burning late in the tower of Lambeth Palace, until in 1549 he finished compiling the *Book of Common Prayer*. The book, which came into use for the first time on Whitsunday that year, was designed so that worshippers could participate in the wording of the service and in the singing of the psalms, rather than remain onlookers throughout. Although the *Book of Common Prayer* has been updated by the *Alternative Service Book* published in 1980, it is still widely used in Anglican churches today.

Cranmer lived a controversial life and died a courageous martyr. He followed Martin Luther's stand against defects in the Church that needed reforming. Though he objected to several Catholic doctrines and leaned towards Protestantism, he neither rejected the Catholic faith outright nor was he happy with the anti-institutionalism and the emphasis on personal religion characteristic of the Reformers. Undoubtedly his influence enabled the Protestant movement to grow.

Sadly, Cranmer showed weakness in his compliance with Henry VIII. He annulled the King's marriage to Catherine of Aragon and three years later he pronounced a similar judgement on his marriage to Anne Boleyn. He also married Henry to, and divorced him from, Anne of Cleves. Prior to this the King had duly rewarded Cranmer for his support by making him Archbishop of Canterbury, an appointment he reluctantly accepted.

Following Henry's death, the nine-year-old Edward became King. Cranmer now moved more firmly in the Protestant direction and pressed forward his reforms. But when the young King died and the Roman Catholic Mary Tudor became Queen she made laws against the Protestants. She hated Cranmer for his part in breaking the marriage of her mother Catherine to the King and for his support of the claims of Lady Jane Grey to be Edward's successor. Mary first condemned him for high treason, then spared his life, but he was subsequently found guilty of heresy. He recanted under threat of the death sentence but later said it was only fear of death and not a change of mind that made him lose courage.

Thomas Cranmer was burned at the stake in

Oxford as were his companions Latimer and Ridley. His courage returned as he thrust his recantations into the fire, and then in shame, the hand that had written them. He died a defiant martyr, criticized to this day for his faults, honoured for his self-sacrifice, and remembered especially for his finest contribution to the Christian world, the *Book of Common Prayer*.

Collect for Advent

Almighty God, give us grace that we may cast away the works of darkness, and put upon us the armour of light, now in the time of this mortal life, in which thy Son Jesus Christ came to visit us in great humility; that in the last day, when he shall come again in his glorious Majesty, to judge both the quick and the dead, we may rise to the life immortal; through him who liveth and reigneth with thee and the Holy Ghost, now and ever. *Amen*.

Collect for Bible Sunday

Blessed Lord, who hast caused all holy Scriptures to be written for our learning: Grant that we may in such wise hear them, read, mark, learn, and inwardly digest them, that by patience and comfort of thy holy Word, we may embrace and ever hold fast the blessed hope of everlasting life, which thou hast given us in our Saviour Jesus Christ. *Amen*.

Collect at Evening Prayer

Lighten our darkness, we beseech thee, O Lord; and by thy great mercy defend us from all perils and dangers of this night; for the love of thy only Son, our Saviour Jesus Christ. *Amen*.

ST IGNATIUS LOYOLA

1491–1556

Founder of the Jesuits

FEAST DAY: *31 July*

Teach us, good Lord, to serve thee as thou deser-
vest; to give, and not to count the cost; to fight,
and not to heed the wounds; to toil, and not to
seek for rest; to labour, and not to ask for any
reward, save that of knowing that we do thy will;
through Jesus Christ our Lord.

This lovely prayer of Ignatius is high on the list of
the Church's treasury of prayers, and is one that
many of us know by heart.

Ignatius was born of the noble Spanish family of
the castle of Loyola, near the Pyrenees. After training at the court of King Ferdinand, he became such
a fine soldier that he was made an officer in the
Spanish Army. But when he was fighting the
French in 1521, a cannonball shattered his right leg
and he lay in hospital for many weeks. It was during his convalescence that he first read a book on
the life of Jesus along with other books on the saints
of the Church. He was so impressed that he threw
away his sword and armour and became a soldier
of Jesus. He replaced his fine clothes with beggars'
rags and went about caring for the poor and sick.
His injury had left him with a permanent limp, but
this did not affect his activities. During a year spent
in prayer and penance, Ignatius wrote his celebrated *Spiritual Exercises*.

Following a visit to the Holy Land, he went to
Barcelona to study Latin and then to Paris to read

philosophy, and there he became friendly with six divinity students, one of whom was St Francis Xavier. In 1534 they took vows of chastity and poverty. They intended to preach in Palestine but were prevented by the war there, so instead they offered their services to the Pope. They were ordained priests, and within three years the company that became known as the 'Society of Jesus', or more commonly, the 'Jesuits', received papal recognition.

The Society, which soon grew in strength, became Christ's army and was organized along strict military lines. Ignatius was their first general. The Jesuits went wherever they were ordered by Rome, and many of them became dedicated missionaries and excellent teachers, setting up schools and colleges. They wore ordinary clothes, but everyone knew they were soldiers of Jesus by their strict discipline and their service to others. When Ignatius died, Jesuit missionaries were to be found all over Europe, as well as in India and even Japan. They were ready to suffer hardship and death in their service for Christ – a truth we see clearly reflected in their founder's most famous prayer.

Lord Jesus Christ,
fill us, we pray, with your light and love,
that we may reflect your wondrous glory.
So fill us with your love
that we may count nothing too small to do for you,
nothing too much to give,
and nothing too hard to bear.

Lord Jesus Christ,
I freely yield to you all my freedom.
Take my memory, my understanding and my will.

All that I have,
All that I am,
All that I shall be, are yours,
and I restore them to you to be used as you will.
Give me only your love and your grace,
and I ask for nothing more.

ST FRANCIS XAVIER

1506–52

Jesuit Missionary

FEAST DAY: *3 December*

When Argentinian pelota players were looking for a patron saint for their team, they chose Francis Xavier, for he is reputed to have played the sport! More in keeping with his extensive travels (although he suffered from seasickness) he is patron saint of tourism, but as one of the greatest Christian missionaries of all time he is also patron saint of Overseas Missions, and of the countries of India, Pakistan and Outer Mongolia.

Francis was born in the castle of Xavier, near Pamplona, Spain, and in his eighteenth year went to the University of Paris, where he became friendly with six serious-minded divinity students led by Ignatius Loyola. Though reluctant at first, he joined them in vowing to live in chastity and poverty and to evangelize the heathen. Three years later they were ordained priests in Venice, and were the first Jesuits to embark on the missionary enterprise that was to be a dominant feature of the Society of Jesus movement.

Francis Xavier was first appointed to accompany Simon Rodriguez to the East Indies, then a Portuguese colony. Honoured by being made apostolic nuncio to the East, he left for India after a year. After a long and hazardous journey he arrived at Goa, which he made his headquarters, and for eleven years he travelled throughout the region and along its coast, teaching, preaching, baptizing and working among the low-caste and poor. Further journeys took him to Ceylon, Malacca, the Molucco Islands and the Malay peninsula. He tried always to learn the native language and was successful in setting up Christian communities wherever he went. Much of his work was spent in undoing the ill treatment of native Christians by unscrupulous European colonists.

He returned to Goa from time to time, and in 1549 he set foot in Japan. With the help of some Japanese converts he succeeded in getting his teaching across and in forming a church that was faithfully to endure persecution. He returned to India after three years, but left within months to fulfil his longing to bring the gospel to China. Sadly, he took ill and died on the way, aged forty-six, worn out with work, but overjoyed at seeing the fruits of his labours. The Jesuits attribute to him over 700,000 converts to Christianity.

Francis Xavier wrote one hymn, which in itself is a prayer – the deeply devotional

My God, I love thee, – not because
I hope for heaven thereby. . .

The hymn dwells on the sufferings of Christ and the love that moved him to die on the cross, and the Christian responds (in keeping with Jesuit conviction):

Not with the hope of gaining aught;
Not seeking a reward. . .

In this prayer we see Francis Xavier's missionary zeal:

O God of all the nations of the earth, remember the multitudes who, though created in your image, do not know you or your Son Jesus Christ their Saviour. Grant that by the prayers and labours of your holy Church they may be delivered from all ignorance and unbelief, and brought to worship you; through him whom you sent to be the Resurrection and the Life of all who trust in you, the same Jesus Christ our Lord.

JOHN CALVIN

1509–64

Reformer of Geneva; Theologian

John Calvin was born in Picardy in France, of Catholic parents who intended him for the priesthood. He studied theology at Paris University, but with doubts about his priestly calling, he turned to studying law at Orléans and Bruges. He was a brilliant student, and several times lectured to the class in the absence of the professor.

His love for theology returned. He was much influenced by a group of Protestants and the writings of Martin Luther, and after a spiritual experience in which he believed God was calling him to restore the Church to its original purity, he made his break with Rome.

In danger from persecution, Calvin fled to Basle, where he decided he would spend his time writing, but on a chance visit to Geneva he was persuaded to join a group who were establishing the Reformation there. With the exception of a short break in Strasbourg where he ministered, Geneva became Calvin's city for over a quarter of a century, in an astonishing and not uncontroversial sense.

From his return in 1541 until his death, Calvin virtually ruled Geneva, transforming it from a city of decadence to one of rigid morality based on God's commandments. He imposed strict laws against all forms of merrymaking, and punished those who stayed away from church and any who disputed biblical or doctrinal authority. He built new schools and a university, encouraged industry at all levels and fostered Protestant ecumenism.

Some see Calvin as 'the dictator of Geneva'. He deserves criticism, as do other excessively religious enthusiasts who enforce religious belief and practice, but criticism alone does him an injustice. He was a hard leader in hard times, but was also capable of warm friendship. He honoured God so much that he hated offence against him and any disregard for his word in the Bible. God, he believed, was sovereign over the whole of life, and requires from us high moral standards, and that is something we ought not to forget. We have inherited a priceless treasure in his biblical commentaries and his *Institutes* in particular, and in Calvinist spirituality with its teaching on the Church and the sacraments, on discipline and prayer. Calvin's contribution not only to the Reformed Church, but to the Church as a whole, is incalculable.

Most gracious God, our heavenly Father,
in whom alone dwells all fullness of light and wisdom:
enlighten our minds, we pray, by your Holy Spirit in
the true understanding of your Word. Give us grace
that we may receive it with reverence and humility.
May it lead us to put our whole trust in you alone, and
so to serve and honour you that we may glorify your
holy name and uplift others by a good example.

Save us, Lord, from being self-centred in our
prayers, and teach us to remember to pray for others. May
we be so bound up in love with those for whom we pray,
that we may feel their needs as acutely as our own, and
intercede for them with sensitivity, with understanding
and with imagination. We ask this in Christ's name.

Let our chief end, O God, be to glorify you,
and to enjoy you for ever.

ST TERESA OF AVILA

1515–82

Carmelite Nun and Mystic

FEAST DAY: *15 October*

> Christ has no body now on earth but yours; no
> hands but yours, no feet but yours; yours are the
> eyes through which his love looks out to the
> world; yours are the feet with which he goes
> about doing good; yours are the hands with
> which he blesses men now.

Teresa, who penned these lovely words, was born
of an influential family in the Spanish town of
Avila, near Madrid. From her earliest years she was
drawn to Christianity, and at the age of twenty-one
became a Carmelite nun. When she was forty-five,
the bishop allowed her to form a convent of her
own. The new order she founded became known as
the 'Discalced Carmelites' because their feet were
uncovered except for rough sandals. Rules were
strict, and the nuns lived on simple vegetarian food
and had no personal possessions at all. Her convents grew in popularity, but she insisted on
restricting the numbers in each to twenty-one –
'experience has taught me what a house full of
women is like!' As a result, her convents were always places of peace and happiness.

Teresa, in fact, has been deemed the happiest of
all the Church's saints, for she combined personal
holiness and devotion with wit and humour. Her
prayer: 'God deliver us from sullen saints' reflects
her outlook. Her noble upbringing in one of the
most brilliant and romantic periods of Spanish

history came through in all she did in her convent. She adored flowers and perfume, and although in charge, she was never aloof from her nuns, mixing with them even at the kitchen sink. 'God likes to walk among the pots and pipkins', she would say. And always there was laughter. Saintliness for her did not lie in dullness or unnatural piety.

Courage was also a feature of her life. In spite of frequent illness, she travelled for miles by horse and cart, establishing and visiting her convents. She braved the heat of summer and the bitter cold of winter, crossing swollen rivers and staying at inns where there was little comfort. On one pilgrimage, when she was elderly and crippled, she and her friends found their way blocked by a fast-flowing and dangerous river. She told her companions: 'I will cross first to see if it is safe. If I am drowned, you are on no account to attempt it.' Her courage brought her safely to the opposite bank.

Teresa's spiritual insight is preserved for us in three books, *The Way of Perfection*, *Foundations* and *The Interior Castle*. These show her to be a woman of great depth of thought and devotion, and a true mystic, but one with her feet firmly on the ground and her heart filled with love. It was said of Teresa, 'To her the religious life was a poem and a song, a thing of light and beauty, of laughter on the edge of tears, and music born of sorrow.'

It is a comfort, Lord, to know that you did not entrust the fulfilment of your will to one so pitiable as me. I would have to be very good, Lord, if the accomplishment of your will were in my hands. Although my will is still self-centred, I give it, Lord, freely to you.

O Lord, by your wisdom, control all things and let me serve you not as I choose but as you will. Let self die in me that I may serve you; let me live to you, for you are life itself.

Helper of all who seek your help, should I keep silent about my needs, hoping that you will meet them? Surely not, for you, my Lord, my joy, knowing how many they are and how you can assist us when we speak of them, bid us pray to you, and affirm that you will never fail to provide.

ST JOHN OF THE CROSS

1542–91

Mystic; Poet; Co-Founder of the Discalced Carmelites

FEAST DAY: *14 December (formerly 24 November)*

Love joins the soul with God, and the more love
the soul has, the more strongly it enters into God
and centres in him.

The words of this beloved saint typify his life and
faith, for he was full of love. In one of his prayers he
reflected of God, 'How delicately thou teachest love
to me!'

Born the son of a poor weaver of noble origin,
John went on to become a Carmelite monk, but
growing disillusionment with the laxity of his order
led to a period of personal uncertainty. He thought
of joining the Carthusians, instead he met the
devoted but cheerful Teresa of Avila – a meeting
that proved decisive for him. She persuaded him to
join the first of her reformed houses for friars,
where he became John of the Cross.

He and his companions lived in simple austerity.
A little wooden cross to which was fastened a paper
figure of Christ is said to have produced more devotion than if it had been an elaborate crucifix.
Their sleeping quarters gave them barely enough
room to lie down and they suffered badly from the
cold. But Teresa, although delighted with their
work, urged them not to be too austere: 'I was
afraid lest the devil should find means of bringing
them to their graves before the work was fully
completed.'

John of the Cross suffered much at the hands of

the unreformed Order of Carmelites. They objected to his reforming zeal, and had him shut up in solitary confinement for eight months before he managed to escape. The conditions were appalling, but it was there that he wrote some of his finest poetry, including 'The Dark Night of the Soul', and possibly, 'The Living Flame of Love'. In a dream he believed he heard Jesus say to him, 'John, what recompense do you ask for your labours?' to which he replied, 'None, my Lord, save that I may suffer and be condemned for your love.'

Though of great spiritual stature, he was full of common sense – due, no doubt, to St Teresa's influence. Like her he was critical of divine visions and revelations, and disliked the overuse of images which could be idolatrous. Nor did he have much time for pilgrimages; 'I should advise staying at home ... Many become pilgrims for recreation more than for devotion.'

John of the Cross is a good example to us who too often grow slack in our spiritual devotion, and to others of us who become too pious and overburdened with religion.

My spirit is dry within me because
it forgets to feed on you.

O sweetest love of God, too little known,
he who has found thee is at rest.
Let everything change O my God, that we may rest in thee.
Everywhere with thee O my God,
everywhere all things with thee as I wish.
O my God, all for thee, nothing for me.
Nothing for thee, everything for me.
All sweetness and delight for thee, none for me.
All bitterness and trouble for me, none for thee.

O my God, how sweet to me thy presence who art the
  sovereign good!
I will draw near to thee in silence and will uncover thy
  feet,
that it may please thee to unite me with thyself,
making my soul thy bride.
I will rejoice in nothing till I am in thine arms.
O Lord, I beseech thee, leave me not for a moment
because I know not the value of my soul.

LANCELOT ANDREWES

1555–1626

Bishop of Winchester; Linguist

Christians who appreciate the beauty of church worship, particularly Anglican, have an affinity with, and owe much to, Lancelot Andrewes. In the *Pictorial History of Winchester Cathedral*, where he was Bishop for seven years, we are told he 'had a great zeal for all which concerned the beauty of holiness'. The orderliness of liturgy and ceremonial in worship, particularly in the Eucharist, was of great importance to him.

Behind such meticulousness was a man steeped in prayer – he was said to spend five hours every day on his knees. In his book *Private Devotions*, a diary of private prayer, we find among his prayers of worship and intercession outpourings of deep penitence and petitions for immunity from worldly corruption. In a familiar prayer he asks:

Forgive me my sins, O Lord;
forgive me the sins of my youth and the sins of
    my age,
the sins of my soul and the sins of my body,
my secret and my whispering sins, my
    presumptuous and my crying sins,
the sins that I have done to please myself, and
the sins that I have done to please others.
Forgive me those sins which I know,
and those sins which I know not;
forgive them, O Lord, forgive them all of thy
    great goodness.

Prior to Winchester, Lancelot Andrewes had been Bishop of Chichester and of Ely, and before that Dean of Westminster. A graduate and a Cambridge don, he was a fine scholar, with mastery of fifteen languages. He was one of the translators of the Authorised Version of the Bible, and worked on the Old Testament books up to 2 Kings. His scholarship and preaching skills were held in high esteem by King James I, and many look back on him as one of the outstanding preachers of his day.

One comment from his time speaks volumes of this man of learning, eloquence and devotion: 'In the schools he was "Dr Andrewes", in the pulpit "Bishop Andrewes", but in his chamber "St Andrewes".'

> We commend unto thee, O Lord,
> our souls and our bodies,
> our minds and our thoughts,
> our prayers and our hopes,
> our health and our work,
> our life and our death;
> our parents and brothers and sisters,
> our benefactors and friends,
> our neighbours, our countrymen,
> and all Christian folk
> this day and always.

Lord Jesus,
I give you my hands to do your work.
I give you my feet to go your way.
I give you my eyes to see as you do.
I give you my tongue to speak your words.
I give you my mind that you may think in me.
I give you my spirit that you may pray in me.

Above all,
I give you my heart that you may love in me,
your Father, and all mankind.
I give you my whole self that you may grow in me,
so that it is you, Lord Jesus,
who live and work and pray in me.

Let this day, O Lord, add some knowledge or good deed
to yesterday.

JOHN DONNE

1571/2–1631

Dean of St Paul's; Metaphysical Poet

John Donne was born in London, the son of a merchant. He studied at Oxford and Cambridge, and began reading law at Lincoln's Inn. He renounced Roman Catholicism when he was nineteen, and joined the Church of England, though not with an easy conscience.

He went with Essex and Raleigh to Cadiz and the Azores, and led a reckless and worldly life for some years. He was dismissed from his post as secretary to the Lord Chancellor because of his secret marriage to his master's wife's niece. This left him penniless and dependent upon charity, but eventually he overcame his frustration at not being able to hold a job, and also his spiritual struggle, and entered holy orders. There followed a royal chaplaincy, a living at Huntingdon, and a rectorship at Sevenoaks. He was later made preacher at Lincoln's Inn, and then, in 1621, Dean of St Paul's, where he exercised a powerful preaching ministry.

In itself John Donne's career was unexceptional, and he might well have been forgotten but for his poetry and deep thoughts of God. As a poet he is deemed the founder of what Dr Johnson called the 'metaphysical' poets. In character he was sensual and worldly, but fervently devotional – more so following the death of his wife. Death, in fact, and a deep sense of personal sinfulness, come through in much of his poetry, which is often obscure but contains precious spiritual insights. Many of us will recall his now familiar lines: 'No man is an island entire of itself . . . Any man's death diminishes me, because I am involved in mankind, and therefore never send to know for whom the bell tolls; it tolls for thee.'

What we write reflects what we are. John Donne's works are said to 'reflect the troubled soul of their author, torn between earthly desires and heavenly aspirations.' The comment fits many a saint – perhaps even us.

His best-known prayer, in which he anticipates the afterlife, reflects his contemplative spirit:

Bring us, O Lord God, at our last awakening into the house and gate of heaven, to enter into that gate and dwell in that house, where there shall be no darkness nor dazzling, but one equal light; no noise nor silence, but one equal music; no fears nor hopes, but one equal possession; no ends nor beginnings, but one equal eternity; in the habitations of thy glory and dominion, world without end.

O Lord, never suffer us to think that
we can stand by ourselves, and not need thee.

O eternal and most gracious God, the
God of security, and also the enemy of security, who
would always have us sure of thy love, and yet would
always have us doing something for it, let me always so
hold on to thee, as present with me, and yet to follow
after thee, as though I had not held on to thee.

Keep us, Lord, so awake in the duties of
our calling that we may sleep in thy peace and wake in
thy glory.

GEORGE HERBERT

1593–1633

Country Clergyman and Devotional Poet

George Herbert came of a noble family. His education at Westminster School and Trinity College, Cambridge set him on course for a prominent career. His appointment as Public Orator at the University brought him in touch with important people, and he became a close friend of James I. Life was exciting and full of promise.

The death of two patrons and of the King himself, together with the influence of a friend, Nicholas Ferrar, turned him from worldly ambitions toward the Church. He had always been religious, but it took an arduous struggle of faith before he submitted himself for ordination in 1630. He was a parish priest for only three years – at Bemerton, near Salisbury – before his death from tuberculosis at the age of forty. From University Public Orator to country parish parson – the contrast was spectacular, but he loved every minute of his Bemerton days, and so endeared himself to his people that he gained the reputation of a model pastor.

George Herbert loved music and was an accomplished flute and viol player. He went twice daily to Salisbury Cathedral to enjoy its music and to pray, declaring, 'It is like heaven to be there.' Uplifted, he returned to his church and parish, conducting its worship with rare dignity and exercising loving pastoral care.

He is, of course, remembered for more: as a writer and poet. His book, *A Priest to the Temple: or the*

Country Parson, portrayed in homely style the ideal English clergyman – temperate, well-read, prayerful and devoted to his flock. George Herbert has been described as 'England's principal devotional poet', and his writings exude a quiet, gentle reverence, drawing us through the countryside he loved and the Church he adorned into the very presence of God. He wrote hymns that are still widely sung today: 'Let all the world in every corner sing'; 'King of Glory, King of Peace'; 'Teach me, my God and King'. They, like most hymns, are prayers in themselves as are his poems, for example:

The shepherds sing; and shall I silent be?
My God, no hymn for thee?
My soul's a shepherd too; a flock it feeds
Of thoughts, and words, and deeds;
The pasture is thy word; the streams, thy grace
Enriching all the place.
Shepherd and flock shall sing, and all my powers
Out-sing the daylight hours.

Love bade me welcome; yet my soul drew back,
 Guilty of dust and sin.
But quick-eyed Love, observing me grow slack
 From my first entrance in,
Drew nearer to me, sweetly questioning,
 If I lacked anything.

'A guest,' I answered, 'worthy to be here.'
 Love said, 'You shall be he.'
'I, the unkind, ungrateful? Ah, my dear,
 I cannot look on thee.'
Love took my hand, and smiling did reply,
 'Who made the eyes but I?'

'Truth, Lord, but I have marred them; let my shame
    Go where it doth deserve.'
'And know you not', says Love, 'who bore the blame?'
    'My dear, then I will serve.'
'You must sit down', says Love, 'and taste my meat.'
    So I did sit and eat.

Thou hast given so much to me:
Give one thing more – a grateful heart, for Christ's sake.

A minister's prayer

Lord Jesus, teach me, that I may teach them;
sanctify and enable all my powers, that in their full
strength I may deliver thy message reverently, readily,
faithfully, and fruitfully. Make thy word a swift word,
passing from the ear to the heart, from the heart to life
and conversation; that as the rain returns not empty, so
neither may thy word, but accomplish that for which it
is given. O Lord, hear; O Lord, forgive; O Lord,
hearken; and do so for thy blessed Son's sake.

RICHARD BAXTER

1615–91

Puritan Divine

A statue of Richard Baxter stands today in the centre of Kidderminster, where traffic merges from all directions – a fitting place for the town's most famous incumbent whose all-embracing faith rebuked the intolerant minds of Church and State.

Richard Baxter was born at Rowton in Shropshire, in the troubled times of conflict between King and Parliament on the one hand, and Church and Dissenters on the other. In the early part of the Civil War he was in sympathy with the Parliamentarians and served in Cromwell's army as chaplain, but he was a man of peace and hated war. He distrusted Cromwell as a good man corrupted by power, and he disliked his religious views. He was ostracized and imprisoned for his 'Nonconformist' leanings, and towards the end of his life suffered at the hands of the cruel and cynical Judge Jeffreys.

Ordained deacon by the Bishop of Worcester, Richard Baxter was appointed 'lecturer' (a parson without freehold) to Kidderminster's parish church. The congregation was sparse when he went there, but in no time the church was crowded with worshippers drawn by Baxter's powerful preaching and pastoral care. Although he always loved the Church of England he was increasingly at odds with it over matters of internal corruption, the question of episcopacy, and its harsh treatment of Dissenters, some of whom he had come to know personally and whose cause he felt able to support. He declined the bishopric of Hereford, and, with great sorrow, withdrew from the Church in 1662 – just three months ahead of the passing of the Act of Uniformity that resulted in 2,000 ministers being thrown out of their livings.

Richard Baxter became spokesman for the moderate or 'Presbyterian' Nonconformists. He looked for some form of 'comprehension' that would assist the return of the Presbyterians and Independents to the Church of England. He advocated moderation at all levels of church life, and extended Christian fellowship across denominational barriers, and in this we see him as an ecumenist ahead of his time. He was a prolific author and is said to have written some 200 works, including *The Reformed Pastor* and *The Saints' Everlasting Rest*. He also wrote several hymns which we still sing today.

Richard Baxter gave us a prayer for the Church in which we see his longing for unity:

Grant more of your Spirit to all
your churches and servants in the world: that as their
darkness and selfishness and imperfections have
defiled and divided and weakened them, and made
them scandalous and harsh toward unbelievers, so
may their knowledge, self-denial and impartial love
truly reform, unite and strengthen them: that the glory
of their holiness may win an unbelieving world to
Christ.

We thank you for all your mercies to our
souls and bodies this night, and all our days and nights:
for our rest and safety, and this morning's light. Cause
us to spend this day in your fear and faithful service.

Preserve our souls from sin, and our bodies from all dangers or hurt which would hinder us from your service. Cause us to live as in your presence, and let us do all to please you, and to your glory, and to the good of our own souls and of one another: and let your love and praise and service, be our continual delight; for Jesus Christ's sake, our Saviour and Intercessor at your right hand.

JOHN BUNYAN

1628–88

Dissenting Preacher and Writer

> As I walked through the wilderness of this world,
> I lighted on a certain place where there was a den
> ... I dreamed, and behold I saw a man clothed
> with rags ...

So begins John Bunyan's *Pilgrim's Progress*, acclaimed the most popular book ever written, apart from the Bible. Full of metaphor and allegory, it depicts the journey of the Christian soul through its earthly experiences of trial and temptation, joys and sorrows, until it reaches its destiny and reward in the Celestial City.

John Bunyan was born at Elstow in Bedfordshire, and became a tinsmith or 'tinker' like his father. He served in the Parliamentary Army during the Civil War, and on returning home he married and underwent a profoundly emotional experience of sin and repentance, which he describes in *Grace Abounding to the Chief of Sinners*. From that moment he saw life as a spiritual warfare in which personal salvation mattered most of all. His appointment as Pastor of Bedford's Independent Congregation gave him a pulpit from which to preach his powerful sermons. Sin, hell, predestination and the wrath of God were prominent features of his preaching, including invective against Roman Catholicism, yet, paradoxically, he celebrated God's abounding grace and love towards sinners.

What freedom Nonconformists enjoyed under

Cromwell was soon reversed with the restoration of the monarchy under Charles II. The Act of Uniformity, passed in 1662, brought severe hardship to dissenting ministers, but even before that a law was in force prohibiting meetings for worship outside the Parish Church. For his refusal to conform, John Bunyan was imprisoned in Bedford jail for twelve years, greatly missing his wife and children.

While in prison he wrote extensively, including the first part of *Pilgrim's Progress*. On his release he worked among the Independents in Bedford and elsewhere, but was imprisoned again for a short period. Like the apostle Paul before him, Bunyan turned captivity into opportunity, witnessing for Christ through his writings, thus providing an example and encouragement to many across the years. Indeed, if he had not been imprisoned, he probably would not have given us his priceless book. Strange, indeed, are the ways of God in human events!

Within a year of Bunyan's death the Toleration Act gave at least conditional freedom of worship to Dissenters. God's Bedford pilgrim had not laboured in vain.

O thou whose name is Emmanuel, our Lord and Sovereign: grace is poured into thy lips, and to thee belong mercy and forgiveness, though we have rebelled against thee. We, who are no more worthy to be called thy servants, beseech thee to do away our transgressions. We confess that thou mightest cast us away for them, but do it not for thy name's sake. Our wisdom is gone, our power is gone, nor have we what we may call our own but sin, shame, and confusion of face for sin. Take pity upon us, O Lord, take pity upon us, and save us. Amen.

JOHN WESLEY

1703–91

Founder of Methodism

To John Wesley is credited the prayer 'O Lord, let us not live to be useless, for Christ's sake.' Few have lived more useful lives!

John, the son of a clergyman, was born at Epworth Rectory in Lincolnshire. One night the thatched roof of the rectory caught fire, and he was the last of the large family to be rescued. His mother saw this as a sign that God wanted him for a special task, and John always saw himself as 'a brand snatched from the burning.'

He went from school to Oxford University, and on becoming a clergyman himself returned to Epworth to assist his father. Later, back at Oxford, he became the leader of a religious group of students which his brother Charles helped to form. They pursued Christian studies, met for Communion services and visited prisoners in Oxford jail. They were first called 'The Holy Club' and then 'Methodists' because of their methodical and disciplined spiritual life.

Both Charles and John eventually went as missionaries to the new colony of Georgia, where they laboured unstintingly, but with little success. On their return to England they met up with a Moravian Christian leader whose deep commitment to Christ challenged their spiritual lethargy, and as a result, both brothers underwent a 'conversion'.

While paying a reluctant visit to an Anglican 'society' meeting in Aldersgate Street in London,

John listened to a reading on Luther's preface to the Epistle to the Romans, and was mentally and spiritually changed. He wrote: 'About a quarter before nine . . . I felt my heart strangely warmed. I felt I did trust in Christ, Christ alone for salvation; and an assurance was given me that he had taken away my sins, even mine, and saved me from the law of sin and death.'

From John's conversion on 24 May 1738 to his death fifty-three years later, he never ceased working. He travelled a quarter of a million miles or more on horseback, preached over 40,000 sermons, wrote well over two hundred books and kept a daily journal. Most of his preaching was to vast congregations in the open air, because Anglican churches were now closed to him. His preaching had a profound effect, especially on the so-called lower and middle classes, and helped to change their outlook and improve their conditions. He trained lay preachers to follow up his evangelistic work, which also took root in America, and today the Methodist Church is at work all over the world.

Forgive them all, O Lord:
our sins of omission and our sins of commission;
the sins of our youth and the sins of our riper years;
the sins of our souls and the sins of our bodies;
our secret and our more open sins;
our sins of ignorance and surprise,
and our more deliberate and presumptuous sins;
the sins we have done to please ourselves
and the sins we have done to please others;
the sins we know and remember,
and the sins we have forgotten;
the sins we have striven to hide from others
and the sins by which we have made others offend;

forgive them, O Lord, forgive them all for his sake,
who died for our sins and rose for our justification,
and now stands at thy right hand to make intercession for us,
Jesus Christ our Lord.

Fix thou our steps, O Lord, that we stagger
not at the uneven motions of the world, but steadily go
on to our glorious home; neither censuring our journey
by the weather we meet with, nor turning out of the
way for anything that befalls us. The winds are often
rough, and our own weight presses us downwards,
Reach forth, O Lord, thy hand, thy saving hand, and
speedily deliver us.

Teach us, O Lord, to use this transitory life
as pilgrims returning to their beloved home; that we
may take what our journey requires, and not think of
settling in a foreign country.

Deliver me, O God, from a slothful mind, from
all lukewarmness, and all dejection of spirit. I know
these can only deaden my love to thee; mercifully free
my heart from them, and give me a lively, zealous,
active and cheerful spirit; that I may vigorously perform
whatever thou commandest, thankfully suffer whatever
thou choosest for me, and be ever ardent to obey in all
things thy holy love.

JOHN HENRY NEWMAN

1801–90

Tractarian Leader and later Cardinal

In the summer of 1833 John Henry Newman was a passenger on board a cargo boat that was becalmed for a week between the islands of Corsica and Sardinia. In the unexpected respite he is said to have penned his famous hymn, 'Lead, kindly Light, amid the encircling gloom, Lead thou me on.' It was the prayer of an unsettled soul.

Newman was thirty-two at the time, and vicar of St Mary the Virgin, Oxford. He had been a committed evangelical, much influenced by his upbringing and the writings of John Calvin. But during his studies at Oxford, and later as Fellow of Oriel College, he had turned from evangelicalism to liberalism. In addition there was the persuasive influence of John Keble, who directed his thinking to the early Church Fathers and the 'catholic' nature of the Church.

In his hymn, which he first published as a poem entitled 'The Pillar of Cloud', he likened himself to the Israelites journeying through the desert, led each step of the way by the light of God's presence. The phrase 'lead thou me on' occurs five times in the poem; it is the burden of his prayer for God's guidance in his present turmoil, and one that was to be meaningful for the rest of his life.

Returning home, Newman became the leader (with John Keble and Edward Pusey) of the Oxford Movement. This was a revival within the Church of England which aimed at rediscovering its tradition from the Early and Medieval Church. It stressed the importance of the priest's role and placed a new emphasis on symbolism and ceremonial in worship and on the Real Presence of Christ in the eucharist. Its leaders had a deep sense of the holiness of God and the mystery of the gospel. Newman's powerful sermons at St Mary's and his *Tracts for the Times*, which extolled Anglicanism and repudiated much in Roman Catholicism, had a wide and lasting appeal. At that time he saw the Church of England as the middle way between Protestantism and Roman Catholicism. But from 1839 he began having serious doubts about the Anglican Church. He went to live for a while in the nearby village of Little-more, where he set up a semi-monastic house, and in due course, having resigned from St Mary's and given up Anglicanism, he was received into the Roman Catholic Church, which he had now come to believe was the true Church. Here he remained and was made a Cardinal, but he was controversial to the last – representative of many, perhaps of us, whose faith is pilgrim and nomadic, unable to settle in this world.

For all his turmoil of spirit (or because of it), John Henry Newman left us a profound insight into God and the life of prayer. What the pulse is to the body, so is prayer to the spirit: intercessory prayer bridges the gap between the self and others. And one of the loveliest prayers ever written is his arrangement of Lancelot Andrewes' prayer:

O Lord, support us all the day long of this troublous life, until the shadows lengthen, and the evening comes, and the busy world is hushed, the fever of life is over, and our work is done. Then, Lord, in thy mercy, grant us and those we love safe lodging, a holy rest, and peace at the last, through Jesus Christ our Lord.

Newman's other spiritual legacy is his celebrated poem, *The Dream of Gerontius*. Set to the music of Edward Elgar, it envisages the righteous soul leaving the body at death and conversing with the angels. Two of his poems have their setting in the well-known hymns 'Praise to the holiest in the height' and 'Firmly I believe and truly'.

O Lord, I give myself to you. I trust you wholly. You are wiser than I, more loving to me than I myself. Deign to fulfil your high purposes in me whatever they be; work in me and through me. I am born to serve you, to be yours, to be your instrument. Let me be your blind instrument. I ask not to see, I ask not to know, I ask simply to be used.

Lord, you are the living flame, burning ceaselessly with love for man. Enter into me and inflame me with your fire so that I might be like you.

Teach me to show forth your praise, your truth, your will. Make me preach you without preaching – not by words, but by my example and by the catching force, the sympathetic influence, of what I do – by my visible resemblance to your saints, and the evident fullness of the love which my heart bears to you.

DAVID LIVINGSTONE

1813–73

Missionary and Explorer

In January 1871 the *New York Herald* sent a reporter, H.M. Stanley, to Africa in search of David Livingstone, of whom nothing had been heard for four years. Stanley's nervous greeting of the famous explorer – 'Dr Livingstone, I presume' – is now a classic among casual remarks!

Before that meeting at Ujiji on Lake Tanganyika, Livingstone had spent thirty-one years traversing Africa on foot. He was to trek another two years before death overtook him at Ilala as he knelt at his bed in prayer. In all he travelled more than 33,000 miles of Africa, mapping the journey as he went and encountering unbelievable difficulties. He was, by any standard, one of the most determined and courageous men who ever lived, and a truly committed Christian.

David Livingstone was born at Blantyre, Scotland, of poor parents, and started work in a cotton mill when he was ten. But his sights were on higher things. By self-education and attendance at evening classes, he entered college, qualified as a medical doctor, and offered for service with the London Missionary Society. He arrived in South Africa in 1840, where he joined Robert Moffat, whose daughter Mary he married. Africa's interior beckoned, and he set out on a series of incredible journeys during which he was mauled by a lion and constantly suffered from malaria and dysentery. He crossed the Kalahari

Desert and explored the region. He penetrated north west into Makololo territory, and from there set out by canoe, following the Zambesi river to the west, finally reaching the west coast of Africa. He then followed the Zambesi eastwards, becoming the first European to find the mighty Victoria Falls which he named, and reached the Indian Ocean. He had crossed the entire continent. Further journeys continued up to his death, expressing his unrelenting urge to 'go forward', as he put it. The cruel effects of the slave trade which he witnessed hurt him terribly, and nothing stopped his determination to oppose it.

David Livingstone's love for the African people was the extension of his love for Christ. A brilliant explorer, he was above all a missionary who aimed to bring the light of the gospel to the souls of that dark land. In all his endeavours he was upheld, he said, by the promise of Jesus, 'Lo, I am with you alway, even unto the end of the world.'

Two of Livingstone's prayers reflect his unwavering commitment to the will of Christ:

O Lord, I am thine. Do what seemeth good in thy sight,
and give me complete resignation to thy Will.

O Jesus, fill me with thy love now, and I beseech thee,
accept me, and use me a little for thy glory. O do, do, I beseech thee, accept me and my service, and take thou all
the glory.

David Livingstone's embalmed body was lovingly carried by devoted African servants 1500 miles to a waiting ship, and on reaching London was buried in Westminster Abbey. His epitaph reads:

Brought by faithful hands
over land and sea
here rests
David Livingstone
Missionary, Traveller,
Philanthropist.

Look upon me, Spirit of the living God,
and supply all thou seest lacking. Soul and body, my
family and thy cause, I commit all to thee. . . Gracious
Almighty Power, I hide myself in thee through thy
Beloved Son. Take my children under thy care. Purify
them and fit them for thy service. Let the Sun of
Righteousness produce spring, summer and harvest in
them for thee . . .

My Jesus, my King, my All, I again
dedicate my whole self to thee. Accept me, and grant, O
gracious Father, that ere this year is gone I may finish
my task . . .

FLORENCE NIGHTINGALE

1820–1910

Nurse of Crimea

When seventeen-year-old Florence Nightingale told her well-to-do parents that she believed God was calling her to become a nurse, they were indignant. In their view respectable girls shunned that kind of work: 'We are ducks that have hatched a wild swan,' they said bitterly.

But nothing daunted her. She trained and qualified, gaining valuable nursing experience in hospitals in Germany, France and Egypt.

The door to her future opened in 1854. At the time Britain and Russia were at war, and as the armies of Britain and France fought in southern Russia the casualties mounted in appalling conditions, and when the call went out for nurses, Florence offered for the Crimea.

She found the situation horrific. The hospital at Scutari, where she established her headquarters, was an old barracks with four miles of corridors. The wounded were arriving at the rate of 4,000 a day, but they stood little chance of recovery in the fever-infested building. A few doctors and nurses coped bravely with hardly any bandages, medicines or blankets, and food was scarce.

But the 'Lady in Chief', as Florence came to be known, delegated groups of nurses to scrub the wards, organized ward routines and took charge of the food and medical supplies when they arrived. The transformation was amazing, lifting the morale of the wounded and aiding their recovery.

Florence regarded all the patients as her family, and the men grew to love her, one of them telling her 'You are Christ to me'. Because she went about the wards at night with her lantern she came to be known as 'the lady with the lamp'. Back in England after the war she was famous. Queen Victoria gave her a brooch inscribed with the words of Jesus, 'Blessed are the merciful', and Parliament donated £50,000 which she used to build a school for the training of nurses. Although unwell for the remainder of her life, she lived to the age of ninety, and was honoured worldwide for her remarkable work at Crimea.

Florence Nightingale's prayer for guidance and dedication

Oh God, you put into my heart this great
desire to devote myself to the sick and sorrowful; I offer
it to you. Do with it what is for your service.
Oh my Creator, are you leading every man of us to
perfection? Or is this only a metaphysical idea for which
there is no evidence? Is man only a constant repetition
of himself? You know that through all these twenty
horrible years I have been supported by the belief (I
think I must believe it still or I am sure I could not
work) that I was working with you who were bringing
every one of us, even our poor nurses, to perfection. O
Lord, even now I am trying to snatch the management
of your world from your hands. Too little have I looked
for something higher and better than my own work –
the work of supreme Wisdom, which uses us whether
we know it or not.

CHARLES HADDON SPURGEON

1834–92

Baptist Preacher and Writer

Those of us who minister to churches as preachers and pastors always hope for an increase in church membership and attendance at services. Few had greater success than Charles Haddon Spurgeon, the famous minister of London's Metropolitan Tabernacle.

Spurgeon had been nurtured in Christianity at his home in Kelvedon, Essex. Both his grandfather and father were Independent ministers. Books such as Bunyan's *Pilgrim's Progress* and Baxter's *Call to the Unconverted* made an impact on his young mind, and during his early teens he began thinking seriously about the state of his own soul, confessing sadness at feeling 'the greatness of my sin without discovering the greatness of God's mercy.'

He made his commitment to Christ during a chance visit to a small Methodist chapel in Colchester, and entered the ministry. He was first appointed to a Baptist chapel near Cambridge, which in the two years he was there saw an enormous growth in the size of the congregation. He was next called, aged nineteen years, to New Park Street, Southwark, for a six-month period: he stayed thirty-eight years. Within twelve months the church was so overcrowded it needed enlarging, and even temporary accommodation in huge assembly halls proved inadequate.

The new Baptist Metropolitan Tabernacle was opened in 1861, and every Thursday evening and twice on Sunday 5,000 people flocked to hear him for the duration of his ministry, and the membership of the church rose to well over that figure.

Spurgeon was a born orator. He also wrote as fluently as he spoke and, like other Calvinist divines, based his message firmly on the Scriptures. He had no room for liberalism, only a clear, doubt-free declaration of salvation by God's grace through personal faith in Christ. In one of his prayers, illustrative of his all-embracing love, he asks:

> Lord, hasten to bring in all thine elect, and then elect some more.

His preaching was balanced by pastoral care for the neighbourhood around his church. The Tabernacle became a focal point of social welfare, and he personally supported the building of a number of almshouses and orphanages. Lord Shaftesbury and Dr Barnardo were his friends, and they greatly valued his help in their work. Whilst he felt the burden of people's physical needs, he never lost sight of the need for that inner change of heart, without which, as he saw it, social change can bear no lasting fruit.

O My Saviour, let me not fall by little and little, or think myself able to bear the indulgence of any known sin because it seems so insignificant. Keep me from sinful beginnings, lest they lead me on to sorrowful endings.

Holiness of life we crave after. Grant that our speech, our thoughts, our actions, may all be holiness, and 'holiness unto the Lord'. We know that there be some that seek after moral virtue apart from God; let us not be of their kind, but may our desire be that everything may be done as unto the Lord, for thou hast said, 'Walk before me and be thou perfect.'

Help us to do so; to have no master but our God; no law but his will; no delight but himself. O, take these hearts, most glorious Lord, and keep them, for 'out of them are the issues of life', and let us be the instruments in thy hand, by daily vigilance, of keeping our hearts, lest in heart we go astray from the Lord our God. Until life's latest hour may we keep the sacred pledges of our early youth.

ST THERESA OF LISIEUX

1873–97

Carmelite Nun

FEAST DAY: *1 October*

Those of us who live ordinary lives will find the saintliness of St Theresa attractive.

In Christian art this beloved Carmelite nun is portrayed holding a bunch of roses symbolizing her promise to 'let fall a shower of roses' of miracles and blessings. Canonized St Theresa of the Child Jesus, she became affectionately known as 'The Little Flower'. Outwardly she lived an undistinguished life, but from the day in her childhood when she felt God calling her to a life of religious obedience, she strove for spiritual perfection. This she believed was attainable not only through severe austerity and self-mortification, but by means of prayer and love.

Theresa was born into a Christian home. Her mother's death when she was four was a shattering blow. The family moved to Lisieux and her father, whom she loved, consented to her entry into the Carmelite convent when she was fifteen. There she became assistant novice-mistress. Ill health prevented her joining other sisters of her Order as missionaries to China, but her missionary zeal was recognized when she became patroness of all foreign missions, with St Xavier, and of all works directed to Russia.

It is unlikely Theresa would have been remembered were it not for her short spiritual autobiography, *The Story of a Soul*, which her convent Superior persuaded her to write. Following Theresa's death from tuberculosis at twenty-four, her book was circulated to other Carmelite convents, winning immediate popularity. It was a book for the ordinary nun by one who loved God in simple ways. She wrote as she lived, commending the life of prayer and love. Everything offered in love, however small, she saw as a gift pleasing to God. She thanked God for all of life, and enjoyed times of fun.

St Theresa pioneered in the 19th-century Church the 'Little Way' – integrity in small things which is possible for all. 'In my little way', she wrote, 'are only very ordinary things. Little souls can do everything that I do.'

Lord Jesus, I am not an eagle.
All I have are the eyes and the heart of one.
In spite of my littleness, I dare to gaze at the sun of love,
and long to fly toward it.
I want to imitate the eagles,
but all I can do is flap my small wings.
What shall I do?
With cheerful confidence I shall stay gazing at the sun
till I die.
Nothing will frighten me, neither wind nor rain.
O my beloved sun, I delight in feeling small
and helpless in your presence;
and my heart is at peace.

WILLIAM TEMPLE

1881–1944

Archbishop of Canterbury

Worship is the submission of all our nature to God.
It is the quickening of conscience by his holiness;
the nourishment of mind with his truth; the purify-
ing of imagination by his beauty; the opening of the
heart to his love; the surrender of will to his purpose – and all of this gathered up in adoration.

These superb thoughts from William Temple's
book *Readings in St John's Gospel* are among his most
familiar, and introduce us to a man of such spiritual
stature and achievement that many rank him
among the finest churchmen of the twentieth century, if not the finest.

William Temple was the second son of Frederick
Temple, Archbishop of Canterbury, and so was
'born in the purple and destined for the purple'.
After schooling at Rugby and a brilliant career at
Oxford, he became a Fellow of Queen's; soon after
he was appointed headmaster of Repton School,
then Rector of St James's Piccadilly and, at only
forty, Bishop of Manchester. Eight years later he
was consecrated Archbishop of York and finally in
1942 Primate of All England, a post which sadly he
held for only two years before his death.

Biographers rightly extol Temple as preacher,
teacher, educationist, evangelist, Church Reformer,
prophet of social righteousness, pioneer of ecumenism, shepherd and pastor of souls. He was all of
these and more.

Between the Piccadilly and Manchester days, Temple (with Dick Sheppard) launched the 'Life and Liberty' movement with its demand for 'liberty without delay' in church and liturgical reform. We mostly owe to him the passing of the Enabling Act which set up the Church Assembly and laid the foundations for the present General Synod and the government of the Church at all levels.

Temple was a pioneer in the Ecumenical Movement, and zealous in his drive to erase the scandal of divisions in the Church. He believed that no one part of the Church of England nor of the Church as a whole enjoyed a monopoly on the truth.

And he was an advocate of the Church's involvement in politics and social concerns. He was deeply bothered by the injustices and inequalities in society, and often jolted the Government of the day to take action. He became the social conscience of England, proclaiming the gospel centred on the incarnation, and he called Christianity 'the most materialistic of all religions,' since it is based on a sound theology of creation, and is rooted in the birth of Christ in our world and on his deep concern for human material needs. For him love and justice were one, and while he was a brilliant scholar, philospher, theologian and prolific writer, he understood ordinary people and had time for them, thus earning him the cherished accolade, 'the people's Archbishop'. The strength of his faith and the warmth of his personality were infectious.

As a preacher, public speaker and broadcaster, few surpassed him. He had no peculiar mannerisms but spoke quietly, without recourse to emotionalism, out of his own deep conviction and experience, invariably leaving his hearers asking 'What does this mean for me?' He spoke in factories and universities alike, and packed every church and hall in which he appeared.

His sudden death sent shock waves throughout the nation and abroad. In 1944 when Britain was strewn with rubble, and lives as well as cities needed rebuilding, the country yearned for him. Someone remarked, on hearing the news of his death, 'God must be very sure of victory when he can take from us a warrior such as William Temple.'

On his grave at Canterbury is inscribed: 'Thou shalt keep him in perfect peace whose mind is stayed on thee.' The text is a fitting one for so great a man, and calls us to trust in God as he did.

A prayer for love

O God of love, we pray thee to give us love:
Love in our thinking, love in our speaking,
Love in our doing,
And love in the hidden places of our souls;
Love of our neighbours near and far;
Love of our friends, old and new;
Love of those with whom we find it hard to bear,
And love of those who find it hard to bear with us;
Love of those with whom we work,
And love of those with whom we take our ease;
Love in joy, love in sorrow;
Love in life and love in death;
That so at length we may be worthy to dwell with thee,
Who art eternal love. *Amen.*

A prayer for unity

O Lord Jesus Christ, who prayed for thy disciples
that they might be one, even as thou art one with the
Father: draw us to thyself, that in common love and
obedience to thee we may be united to one another, in the
fellowship of the one Spirit, that the world may believe
that thou art Lord, to the glory of God the Father. *Amen.*

A prayer of blessing

May the love of the Lord Jesus draw us to himself;
May the power of the Lord Jesus strengthen us in his
service;
May the joy of the Lord Jesus fill our souls;
And may the blessing of God Almighty, the Father, the
Son and the
Holy Ghost, be amongst you and remain with you always.

TOYOHIKO KAGAWA

1888–1960

Japanese Christian and Social Reformer

Few Christians have been more governed and moti-
vated by the cross of Christ than Kagawa of Japan.
In one of his poems he wrote:

As in a single Word,
Christ's Love-Movement is summed up in the Cross.
The Cross is the whole of Christ, the whole of Love.
God speaks to man through the Cross.
Of Love's mysteries concealed in the Divine Bosom.

Such love compelled him to the extremes of self-
sacrifice, and made him one of the most Christ-like
Christians of the twentieth century.

Toyohiko Kagawa was fostered by wealthy rela-
tives, having lost both his parents when he was four
years old. He was seldom happy, and found con-
solation in his loneliness among the birds and
animals. He was a scholarly youngster, and his
foster uncle had ambitious plans for him: but when
Kagawa, under the influence of an American missionary, converted to Christianity from Buddhism
and entered the Christian ministry, he was dis-
inherited and left penniless.

What he saw during his seminary training at
Kobe determined his life's work. On a visit to the
slums of Shinkawa district he saw the desperate
plight of the poor, and decided that the only way to
help them was to live among them. Kobe suffered
every kind of deprivation – overcrowded and
disease-ridden slums, crime and violence – but for

fifteen years, and largely with his wife and children, Kagawa shared the appalling lot of a people he grew to love and serve. He suffered constant ill-health and exhaustion, but nothing daunted his zeal to bring them the gospel of Christ's love. At his conversion he had been moved by Christ's compassion for the needy and his sacrifice on the cross, and every day since he prayed: 'O God, make me like Christ!' Surely his prayer was answered.

His words were supported by deeds, for, like James in the New Testament, he knew that religious words without action were useless in helping the poor and stricken. He founded a Trade Union to protect workers from unscrupulous employers; he forced the government to improve the slum conditions; he shared his meagre food and home, and gave away royalties from his writings, and when an earthquake devastated the Kobe area in 1923 he organized relief work. He opposed Japan's entry into the war, for he was a man of peace, and for this he was arrested.

Kagawa was small in stature, but his heart of love was boundless – like the love of Christ – and a challenge to all aspiring Christians.

Great God, our Father: As we call to mind the scene of Christ's suffering in Gethsemane, our hearts are filled with penitence and shame that we foolishly waste our time in idleness and that we make no progress in the Christian life from day to day . . . We are ashamed that war and lust flourish and grow more rampant every day.

Forgive us for our cruel indifference to the Cross, and pardon us that, like the bystanders of old, we merely stand and gaze in idle curiosity upon the piteous scene. O teach us, we beseech thee, the good news of thy forgiveness.

Cause humanity, degenerate as it is, to live anew, and hasten the day when the whole world shall be born again.

Take Thou the burden, Lord;
I am exhausted with this heavy load
My tired hands tremble,
And I stumble, stumble
Along the way.
Oh, lead with Thine unfailing arm
Again today.

Unless Thou lead me, Lord,
The road I journey on is all too hard.
Through trust in Thee alone
Can I go on.

Yet not for self alone
Thus do I groan;
My people's sorrows are the load I bear.
Lord, hear my prayer –
May thy strong hand
Strike off all chains
That load my well-loved land.
God, draw her close to Thee!

GLADYS AYLWARD

1901–70

Missionary to China

I once had the pleasure of introducing Gladys
Aylward to a huge congregation. After she had
spoken I took her to an overflow meeting in a hall
where the service had been relayed. She was very
short – she was known worldwide as 'The Small
Woman' – and was wearing a tight-fitting Chinese-
style dress. So she asked me to lift her on to the
platform – and that was the moment (of which I
love to tell) when I held Gladys Aylward in my
arms!

She was born in Edmonton, London. She left
school with little education and became a parlour-
maid. On hearing that the China Inland Mission
needed more missionaries in China she decided
that this was to be her work for God. She was accepted for training but was later dismissed as being
unsuitable and unpromising material. Sadly she
returned to her domestic work, but her ambition
remained and was soon to be realized in an incredible way.

In China there was an elderly missionary, Mrs
Jennie Lawson, who had advertised for help.
Gladys offered to come and was accepted, provided
she could find her own way of getting there. This
she did, travelling at her own expense right across
Europe and Russia to China, facing frightening
hazards along the way.

Jennie Lawson lived in a tumbledown house in
Yangcheng, but with Gladys' help the place was

transformed and soon the work of teaching the peasants and muleteers began. On the death of Jennie Lawson, Gladys Aylward was left alone, and there are many stories of her ingenuity and courage as she struggled to teach the Bible and show people the love of God.

And then came the greatest act of bravery. In 1938 Japanese planes attacked the village and many people were killed or maimed. Soldiers followed on foot and Gladys was badly beaten. Later the Japanese offered a sizeable reward for her capture, and it was then that she led 100 orphan children to safety across the mountains and the Yellow River. Her prayers at this time reflect the urgency of the situation and her dependence upon God:

You'll have to help me, Lord . . .
Whichever path I face when I stop, I shall take.
D'you hear me, Lord?
Whichever path I face when I stop turning, I shall go along . . .

It's over to you now, God, I'm finished.
Oh God, do something for us now. Don't let us down.
Help us, God. Get us to the other side of the river.
Oh Lord, get us over the river.

Illness forced Gladys Aylward to return to England after twenty years in China. When she recovered she went to live in Formosa (now Taiwan) and there she died. By then she was world-famous and a film, *The Inn of the Sixth Happiness*, was made, telling the story of her remarkable life.

O God, Here's my Bible! Here's my money!
Here's me!
Use me, God!

O God, give me strength.

If I must die, let me not be afraid of death;
but let there be a meaning, O God, to my dying.

(*Based on a Chinese Prayer*)

DIETRICH BONHOEFFER

1906–45

German Pastor; Theologian; Martyr

Dietrich Bonhoeffer was born at Breslau of Christian parents, and enjoyed a happy family upbringing. He was a fine scholar and theologian, yet also welcomed opportunities of involvement in church and youth work. He was an advocate of ecumenism and travelled widely, gaining experience of church life in Barcelona, London and America. A deeply spiritual man, he became increasingly dependent on the Bible for inner nourishment and guidance. Anyone reading him today, as John Robinson has shown in his famous book *Honest to God*, will find his theological viewpoints thought-provoking. But the real appeal of the man and his writings springs from his resistance to Hitler and Nazism up to and during the Second World War. Most of us take our faith so far: he took his all the way, and for that we honour him as one of the great Christians of the twentieth century.

Bonhoeffer returned to Germany from London in 1935 at the invitation of the German Church to become head of a training college for ministers. It coincided with the dangerous rise to power, as he saw it, of Adolf Hitler and the National Socialist Party. Many German Christians however, supported the movement, and so deep was Bonhoeffer's sorrow at their connivance that, with the support of men like Martin Niemöller and Paul Schneider he set up the Confessing Church, in clear opposition to the Party's fanatical racism. It was an act of outstanding courage which for Bonhoeffer and scores of his companions led to ostracism, imprisonment and death.

He was arrested in April 1943 and kept in prison for eighteen months, with no contact with the outside world except letters to his parents and notes to his friends scribbled on bits of paper. These were collected after the war and published in a book called *Letters and Papers from Prison*.

In September 1944 Bonhoeffer was placed in close confinement in the Gestapo headquarters on suspicion of being involved in the plan to assassinate Hitler. Soon afterwards he was taken to Buchenwald concentration camp and from there to Flossenburg, where he was hanged on 9 April 1945.

The camp doctor, who knew nothing about him at the time, wrote ten years later about the event of which he was an eyewitness:

On the morning of that day . . . through the half-open door in one room of the huts I saw Pastor Bonhoeffer, before taking off his prison garb, kneeling on the floor praying fervently to God. I was most deeply moved by the way this lovable man prayed, so devout and so certain that God heard his prayer. At the place of execution he again said a short prayer, and then climbed the steps to the gallows, brave and composed. His death ensued after a few seconds. In the almost fifty years that I worked as a doctor, I have hardly ever seen a man die so entirely submissive to the will of God.

O God, early in the morning I cry unto you.
Help me to pray and to think only of you;
I cannot pray alone.

In me there is darkness, but in you there is light;
I am lonely, but you do not leave me;
I am feeble in heart, but you are with me;
I am restless, but with you there is peace;
In me there is bitterness, but with you there is patience;
I do not understand your ways, but you know the way
for me.

O heavenly Father, I praise and thank you
for the peace of this night and of this new day;
for all your goodness and faithfulness throughout my life.
You have granted me many blessings;
now let me accept tribulation from your hand.
You will not lay on me more than I can bear;
You make all things work together for good for your
children.

O Holy Spirit, grant me faith that will save me from despair,
from passions and from sin;
grant me such love for you and for men
that will blot out all hatred and malice;
grant me the hope that will release me from fear and
malice.

I remember before you all my loved ones,
my fellow prisoners, and all who in this place
perform their hard service.

Lord, have mercy.
Restore me to liberty,
and help me so to live now
that I may answer before you and all men.
Lord, whatever may happen this day,
may your name be praised.

MOTHER TERESA

1910–

Founder of the Missionaries of Charity

I see Christ in every person I touch because he
has said, 'I was hungry, I was thirsty, I was
naked, I was sick, I was suffering, I was homeless
and you took me. . .' It is as simple as that. Every
time I give a piece of bread, I give it to him. That
is why we must find a hungry one, and a naked
one. That is why we are totally bound to the poor.
When we cleanse the wounds of the poor we are
cleansing the wounds of Christ.

The words are Mother Teresa's and so, more
remarkably, are the actions. She is Christ at work,
the epitome and embodiment of his perfect love. No
sacrifice is too great, no barrier insuperable, no
wound too repulsive. Her work amongst the
world's destitute has graced the latter half of this
twentieth century, rebuking, challenging and in-
spiring others of us who try to follow Christ.

Born in Yugoslavia, Mother Teresa became a
nun at eighteen and, in accordance with her missionary fervour, offered her service to the Bengal
Mission, who sent her to the Irish teaching convent
in Loreto, Calcutta. Then came the 'call within the
call' to serve the poorest of the poor. With a special
dispensation from the Pope and some basic medical training she began her work of helping the sick
and comforting the dying in Calcutta's slums. In a
while she was joined by other sisters from the
Loreto convent, and several high-caste Indian

women who had to overcome their unease at treating low-caste victims.

So began her order of the 'Missionaries of Charity' whose work has spread beyond Calcutta and India to many places in the world where people are lonely, diseased and dying.

Mother Teresa sees loneliness and the feeling of being unwanted as one of the biggest problems in the West. She calls downtrodden and destitute people 'our people', because she knows them to be her own sisters and brothers in Christ, and all children of God.

I once had the pleasure of meeting Mother Teresa. Our conversation was all too brief, we shook hands warmly, and I shall always count it an exceptional privilege, for I knew I had also been in the presence of Christ, which is the hallmark of saintliness.

Make us worthy, Lord, to serve our fellow
men throughout the world who live and die in poverty
and hunger. Give them, through our hands, this day
their daily bread, and by our understanding love, give
peace and joy.

Dearest Lord, may I see you today and every
day in the person of your sick, and, whilst nursing
them, minister unto you.
Though you hide yourself behind the unattractive
disguise of the irritable, the exacting, the unreasonable,
may I still recognize you, and say: 'Jesus my patient,
how sweet it is to serve you.'
Lord, give me this seeing faith, then my work will
never be monotonous. I will ever find joy in
humouring the fancies and gratifying the wishes of all
poor sufferers.

O beloved sick, how doubly dear you are to me, when you personify Christ; and what a privilege is mine to be allowed to tend you.

Sweetest Lord, make me appreciative of the dignity of my high vocation, and its many responsibilities. Never permit me to disgrace it by giving way to coldness, unkindness, or impatience.

And O God, while you are Jesus, my patient, deign also to be to me a patient Jesus, bearing with my faults, looking only to my intention, which is to love and serve you in the person of each of your sick.

Lord, increase my faith, bless my efforts and work, now and for evermore.

MARTIN LUTHER KING

1929–68

Leader of American Civil Rights Movement

Martin Luther King was born the son of a negro Baptist minister in Atlanta, Georgia. As a boy he was saddened to see black and white people kept apart. He intended being a lawyer but chose to follow his father into the ministry, and in 1954 he became the minister of a church in Montgomery, Alabama.

Montgomery had a rule of segregation on buses, and it was an incident in which a black woman refused to give up her seat to a white person that sparked off a boycott of the buses by the city's black population. The boycott, led by Martin Luther King, lasted over a year, and succeeded in overturning the law of segregation.

Martin Luther King, who was by now famous throughout America, led Civil Rights marches in other cities, and eventually became a world figure. In 1964 he was awarded the Nobel Peace Prize.

His campaigns brought bitter opposition from those who favoured segregation and, ironically, from many black people who thought his non-violent protests, in the manner of Mahatma Gandhi, would not get results quickly enough. He and his family were under constant threat. He suffered deep anguish for them and for other followers whose lives were in danger, but he never wavered from his beliefs or aims, often quoting the words of Jesus: 'Love your enemies and pray for your persecutors' (Matt. 5.44 NEB) and his prayer from the cross, 'Father, forgive them; they do not know what they are doing' (Luke 23.34 NEB).

A biographer of Martin Luther King wrote that he put his trust entirely in the force of creative love. He was sure that violence was wrong and counter-productive. By a tragic irony Dr King was the victim of violence – gunned down by a white assassin at Memphis, Tennessee. He was fully pre-pared and had anticipated this in a speech only the day before.

His address at the Lincoln Memorial, Wash-ington, back in August 1963, before a vast crowd ranks as one of the greatest ever made, and remains a most powerful challenge to racism.

> I have a dream that one day on the red hills of Georgia the sons of former slaves and the sons of former slave owners will be able to sit down together at the table of brother-hood ... that my four little children one day will live in a nation where they will not be judged by the colour of their skin, but by the content of their character ... This will be the day when all of God's children ... black men and white men, Jews and Gentiles, Protestants and Catholics, will be able to join hands and sing in the words of the old negro spiritual, 'Free at last! Free at last! Great God Almighty we are free at last'.

Some aspects of the life of Martin Luther King remain controversial, but none of us should doubt his commitment as a servant of Christ to the cause of Civil Rights, and the lasting value of his work. All of history's famous Christians had personal defects, but in spite of them, and indeed because of them, each was 'something of a saint'.

Lord, I am taking a stand for what I believe
is right. The people are looking to me for leadership,
and if I stand before them without strength and
courage, they will falter. I am at the end of my powers.
I have nothing left. I've come to the point where I can't
face it alone.

*His final words as he left his church in Montgomery for the
wider work to which he believed God was calling him*

And now unto Him who is able to keep us
from falling and lift us from the dark valley of despair
to the bright mountain of hope, from the midnight of
desperation to the daybreak of joy; to Him be power
and authority, for ever and ever. Amen.

Epilogue

Almighty God,
You have knit together your elect
into one communion and fellowship
   in the mystical body of your Son.
Give us grace so to follow your blessed saints
in all virtuous and godly living,
that we may come to those unspeakable joys
which you have prepared for those who truly love you;
through Jesus Christ our Lord.

Collect for All Saints' Day, ASB 1980

Sources

Adels, Jill Haak, *The Wisdom of the Saints*. Oxford 1987

Basset, Elizabeth, *Love is my Meaning*. DLT 1973

Bently, James, *A Calendar of Saints*. Orbis 1986

Blythe, Ronald, *Divine Landscapes*. Viking 1986

Bonhoeffer, Dietrich, *Letters and Papers from Prison*. Fontana 1953

A Book of Services and Prayers. Independent Press (now the United Reformed Church) 1959

Bull, Norman, *One Hundred Great Lives*. Hulton 1972

Burgess, Alan, *The Small Woman*. Evans Brothers

Campbell R.J., *Livingstone in Africa*

Campling and David, *Words for Worship*

Castle, Tony, *The Hodder Book of Christian Prayers*. Hodder & Stoughton 1986

Colquhoun, Frank, *New Parish Prayers*. Hodder & Stoughton 1982

Contemporary Parish Prayers. Hodder & Stoughton 1975

CWN Series (British Weekly) 4 May 1973

A Dictionary of Christian Spirtuality. SCM 1983

Doig, Desmond, *Mother Teresa: Her People and Her Work*. Collins 1978

Fosdick, *The Meaning of Prayer*. Fontana 1915

Gill, Frederick, *The Glorious Company*. Epworth Press

Green, Barbara, *God of a Hundred Names*. Gollancz 1962

Harcourt, Giles, and Harcourt, Melville, *Short Prayers for the Long Day*. Collins 1978

Hoagland, Victor, *The Book of Saints*. Regina Press 1986

Iremonger, F.A., *Life of William Temple*. London 1948

Kempis, Thomas à, *The Imitation of Christ*. Everyman 1976

Lee, F.H. *The Children's Book of Saints*. Harrap 1940

Llewelyn, Robert, *The Joy of the Saints*. DLT 1988

Luther, Martin, *The Meaning of Prayer*

Mackinty, Gerard, *Today We Celebrate*. Collins 1985

Milner-White, Eric and Briggs, G.W., eds, *Daily Prayer*. Pelican 1959

Muggeridge, Malcolm, *Something Beautiful for God*. Collins 1972

Northcott, Cecil, *Livingstone in Africa*. World Christian Books

The Oxford Book of Prayers. Oxford University Press 1985

Payne, Robert, *The Christian Centuries*. W.H. Allen 1967

Pennington, Basil, *Through the Year with the Saints*. Image Books 1988

Robertson, Edwin, *The Shame and the Sacrifice*. Hodder 1987

Robinson and Winward, *Prayers for Schools*. Scripture Union 1967

Slack, Kenneth, *Martin Luther King*. SCM Center Books

Temple, William, *Readings in St John's Gospel*. Macmillan 1961

Thompson, Phyllis, *A London Sparrow*. Highland 1984

Trout, Jessie M., *Kagawa, Japanese Prophet*

Weatherhead, Leslie, *A Private House of Prayer*. Hodder & Stoughton 1958

Wyon, Olive, *The School of Prayer*. SCM 1943

Zundel, Veronica, *Famous Prayers*. Lion 1983